Sculpturing
In Clay

Acknowledgments

We wish to express our sincere thanks to Virginia McIntire, John Schofield, Donna Ortlieb, Helen Brush, Floyd Cawthon, and Jack Ruiz for their outstanding photography: to Edward and Dorothy Ancona, Vermel Bellou, Robert and Jane Cheatham, Edmund and Mercedes Penney, Gaye Cox and Helen Kumme, for the loan of art pieces from their collections, and a special thanks to Frances Commons, Olivia Grillo, Peggy Stilton, Dr. F. Carlton Ball, and Kathryn Paulson Grounds who, each in his own way, helped pull this book together.

Sculpturing In Clay

by Janice Lovoos

TAB TAB BOOKS Inc.
BLUE RIDGE SUMMIT, PA. 17214

FIRST EDITION

FIRST PRINTING

Copyright © 1982 by TAB BOOKS Inc.

Printed in the United States of America

Library of Congress Cataloging in Publication Data

Lovoos, Janice.
    Sculpturing in clay.
            2. Ceramics
    1. Pottery craft.   I. Amparan, Joann.
II. Title.
TT920.L68   738.1′4   81-18271
ISBN 0-8306-1344-7 (pbk.)   AACR2

Cover 1 photo courtesy of Tom Kelly.
Cover 4 photo courtesy of John Schofield.

Contents

Introduction

Clay is one of the most versatile of all materials and, to many craftsmen, the most satisfying as a means of aesthetic expression. The grade school student displays with pride his first pinch-pot and gains a sense of achievement. The homemaker creates attractive and functional pieces for the family's use and enjoyment.

The use of clay as a medium of expression is important whether or not the work is completed as a permanent piece. Because clay responds immediately to the artist's touch, he finds it valuable for making "sketches" or maquettes of his own ideas.

Clay is a very personal medium that offers everyone a direct and satisfying way of making his own statement. It is among the most sensitive of materials and once you have experienced rolling it between your fingers, you may find it irresistible. Real clay has a feel unlike any other substance, a tactile quality which cannot be duplicated by Plasticine or other substitutes.

Clay is a practical medium because it does not require a studio or workshop. You need not own a kiln. There are many places where firing may be done for you: a studio workshop, the commercial outlets where you purchase ceramic supplies (as well as the clay itself), at recreational centers, adult educational centers, school or university ceramic departments.

Clay is where you find it—in river beds, in meadows, or even in your own backyard. There is not likely to be a shortage of clay!

Clay is perhaps more closely related to our daily lives than any other craft. Look through the rooms of your home and see how many pieces are made from clay.

In ancient Egypt, Bast, the cat, was the goddess of pleasure and music, the guardian against evil spirits. It was the custom to mummify the bodies of cats; at Beni Hasan, a cat cemetery was discovered. Notice the contemporary lines of this ancient, priceless sculpture, with its gold ring in the right ear.

Look through the pages of history. Why have we learned as much as we have about people who lived hundreds, even thousands of years ago? Because throughout all time, people have made things from clay.

Every culture has contributed to this history by leaving behind a record of pots, jars, vessels, cooking utensils and the like, made from clay, providing priceless resource material for historians and archeologists. How indebted we should be to these early craftsmen!

In the first part of the 29th Century, American crafts were thriving and changing. In the 40s when World War II imposed restrictions on vital materials such as glass, metal, and wood, craftsmen were obliged to find new materials, or new uses for old ones. They became ingenious in the use of clay. The market overflowed with slip-cast pieces, many of them imitations of German and Japanese figurines. Ceramic jewelry was tried to emulate the qualities of more expensive materials. Everyone was turning his garage into a studio and starting a business.

The innovations of these hobbyists were not necessarily good, nor always in good taste, but their inventiveness and enthusiasm inspired others to consider clay as a serious art medium, and California craftsmen led the way.

This book is not intended as an in-depth study of ceramic techniques, nor throwing on the wheel. It does, however, contain sufficient instruction to launch a beginner. It is more than another book on how-to-make-ceramics. It is important as *a book of ideas*.

The work shown on the following pages includes pieces simple enough for the least experienced clay worker to reproduce. It is hoped that some of the more complex pieces may stimulate professional designers and craftsmen to adapt some of these ideas to their own projects or translate them into other materials.

Everything in this book is an original design made by the three artists who sign their work *Clay In Particular*.

Chapter 1

Clay In Particular:
A Unique Approach
to Stoneware

Clay In Particular is the name used by a group which began with three craftsmen blending their talent to create a *different* look in stoneware (Fig. 1-1).

Joann Amparán had modeled in clay from the time she was a girl growing up in Los Angeles. At six, her first clay pieces were the baby Moses in a basket and a basket with loaves and fishes. In junior high school, her art class was given a clay assignment. She modeled a ten-inch figure of a boy playing a guitar. As a teenage baby-sitter, she found herself using plastic modeling clay to make graceful ballerinas to entertain the children. Entering Manual Arts High School, enrollment in the clay art class introduced her to Hazel S. Martin, an excellent teacher, who had been a student of Dr. Glen Lukens. There she learned to model, mix glazes, make plaster molds, and decorate clay pieces.

Her Mexican-born husband Carlos Amparán and his brother Raoul founded Tru-Fyre Laboratories, which first manufactured prepared ceramic underglazes and low-fire glazes for the hobbyist.

The Amparáns had always admired the designs painted spontaneously by Mexican artists. They envisioned these decorations painted on a finer clay body, firing at higher temperatures, but they found that Mexican potters had little interest in doing anything different from what they had been doing for years. Their only concern was making a living.

On a third trip to Mexico the Amparáns revisited Benigno Barron, an outstanding potter who lived in Guanajuato. He was a fine designer who used striking Indian and Spanish Colonial pat-

Fig. 1-1. The three artists who signed their joint artistic efforts *Clay In Particular*. In foreground Joann Amparán, Gonzalo Duran; in background, Benigno Barron. Photographed in their first studio, in front of a catenary kiln Carlos Amparán was building.

terns on the pots he threw rapidly on a kick-wheel. His innovations and ideas had been copied or used by larger manufacturers in Mexico but this gave Benigno no profit.

The idea that there was something wonderful going on among potters outside his own little town appealed to Benigno. He listened with an open mind to what the Amparáns told him about California potters and how they were working in stoneware. A little later he accepted their invitation and came to Los Angeles.

When Carlos learned that Benigno was on his way, he bought a small commercial building with adjoining living quarters.

Production potters, such as Benigno, were used to having a helper who supplied the potters with clay and stood by to take away the finished pots. He would need a "gofer." Joann accepted the job. However, it wasn't long before she became enchanted with the infinite variety of forms he was capable of making; she, too, was soon turning out Lady Flower Holders.

A few weeks after Benigno arrived, the Amparáns visited a modest gallery in Thousand Oaks. The drawings and paintings exhibited had been done by Gonzalo Duran, a young Mexican student who had won a three year scholarship to Chouinard School of Art.

"When Carlos and I walked into that gallery," Joann recalled, "the walls seemed alive with color and motion."

They immediately contacted Gonzalo Duran.

"Have you ever painted on clay?" Joann asked him.

"No," he told her, but he was interested and willing to try. Carlos was eager to encourage Gonzalo and to give him new acrylic color. Benigno's skill on the wheel made a deep impression on the younger artist. Any surface free of decoration was a temptation to Gonzalo. It wasn't long before he was experiencing the thrill of painting on a surface that had been bisque-fired and glazed in preparation for a second firing.

The round forms of pots, vases, bowls and jars, and the round flat surfaces of plates were natural foils for Gonzalo's spontaneous brushwork. The fanciful figures, scrolls, and flowers, so appealing on canvas, proved equally attractive when applied to the rounded forms. As an artist who rarely stops painting and drawing, Gonzalo was especially intrigued with the idea of continuity design going around the form.

His ideas were stimulated by what Benigno threw on the wheel, but Gonzalo knew instinctively how to decorate the pieces. He has a good eye for design. Although he is an original artist, beautifully planned and photographed pages from *Vogue*, Audubon, comic books, fashion magazines, old issues of *LIFE* magazine and children's books—*especially* children's books—offer a constant flow of imagery. He goes to see films for the same reason. His world is made up of imagery.

Benigno and Gonzalo worked easily together from the start of their collaboration. They never discussed what they were going to do—they just did it! This complete rapport and meeting of minds was reflected in their work. Shortly after their meeting Gonzalo moved in with Benigno; Joann started working with them—and that was the beginning of *Clay In Particular!*

Each one fell naturally into the part of the work which he performed best. Benigno was given free reign in throwing on the wheel. Joann began to enlarge her talent for modeling. Gonzalo's gift for painting lent itself beautifully to the clay surface. With this pooling of talents they produced lamp bases, ash trays, casserole dishes, compotes, flower holders, soap dishes, and candle holders. Most of the pieces were in the forms of men. From the start they decided not to accept commercial limitations (Fig. 1-2).

"We wanted products that were unique and handmade, not production-line pieces. Because of the influence of Gonzalo and Benigno, Carlos and I were able to realize this. We called on Carlton Ball, master ceramist and teacher, known to freely share his vast knowledge, generously helping other potters. He came and talked to us, making valuable suggestions. We took an old low-fire Cal-kiln that opened on both ends and inserted new high-fire brick, which enabled us to fire to Cone 10."

Fig. 1-2. An order is being completed as Gonzalo Duran (left) decorates a lamp base with cutout areas. Benigno Barron (center) threw the lamp on the wheel. Here, he is shown using wax resist on the top of a jar. Joann Amparán (right) wets her brush with the tip of her tongue as she models a small figure. In the background is the Cal-kiln which they relined with high-fire brick and used for years, with hundreds of firings at Cone 10 reduction.

"Then we took off," Joann declared, "without regard for what had been done previously. We did not wish to duplicate what others had been doing. Much as we admired individual potters and the Japanese influence among many California potters, our aim was to combine the rich, spontaneous elements of the Mexican pottery with the technically superior stoneware clay fired at high temperatures."

The chief differences in the *Clay In Particular* approach were:

1. A potter, a modeler and a decorator involved creatively on a single piece.

2. Working on clay forms after they have been thrown on the wheel. (Soft clay forms readily slump into natural positions.)

3. Surface decoration. No one was doing elaborate surface decoration at the time; *Clay In Particular* made a strong point of using it.

Through experimentation, they discovered that the low-firing underglaze colors Carlos was manufacturing could be applied on a piece decorated with Cone 10 glazes. The *majolica* technique enabled them to use color (with the exception of red and its derivatives) for colorful patterns.

Over a period of time, other creative people—Michael Frimkers, Gaye Cox, Carlota Malan de Calabria, Matt Leeds, Warren Dunn—wandered in and out of their studio to work for a while. There was a spark of creativity at *Clay In Particular* that drew creative people. An exchange of ideas was constantly spinning off from the varied cultures and backgrounds. Small wonder that originality thrived in this atmosphere!

Chapter 2

Starting to Work

Clay work involves following recipes and formulas. You will discover new uses for familiar tools and utensils used in maintaining a home. Every piece shown in this book might have been made in the corner of a kitchen.

If you have a sturdy workbench in the garage or basement, a durable kitchen table, card table, or counter of a comfortable height, you have a workshop. A breadboard provides a good work surface; so does Formica. If you don't have a usable surface, put down a piece of heavy canvas and work on that. If you have a drawing board or drawing table, so much the better.

How you set up your work area depends on the amount of space available. You'll be surprised at what you can produce in 1½ square feet of space.

TOOLS

To start your work, the following items will be needed:
- [ ] A slender manicure stick
- [ ] Elephant ear or cosmetic sponge
- [ ] Wooden stick with "teeth" (serrated edge)
- [ ] Medium size bowl for water
- [ ] Damp cloth
- [ ] Polyethylene bags

The following tools are also very useful (Fig. 2-1).
- [ ] Rolling pin
- [ ] Manicure stick
- [ ] Paring knife

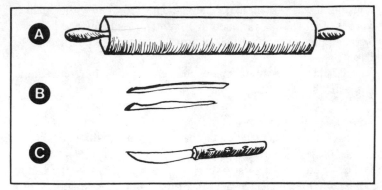

Fig. 2-1. Basic tools. (A) Rolling pin. (B) Manicure sticks. (C) Paring knife.

Whenever a cellulose sponge can be used for clean-up, you will need delicate sponges such as shown in Fig. 2-2.

There may be a local craft or hobby shop nearby, where you can buy professionally designed tools. If you have old modeling tools, they may be sharpened, reshaped, notched, filed down, or honed to a fine point. Keep plenty of small sticks and tools around. You'll find dozens of ways to use them; they may even give you ideas.

You can make your own basic tools (Fig. 2-3). At *Clay In Particular,* they found an old modeling tool to be one of the most

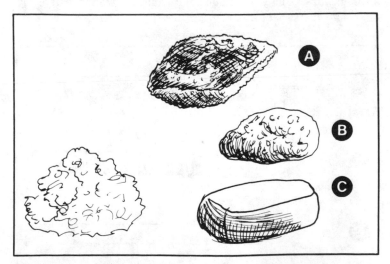

Fig. 2-2. Sponges. (A) Elephant ear—flat, fine sponges. (B) Cosmetic or silk sponge, fine and soft.(C) Mediterranean sponge or large bath sponges for bigger pieces.

valuable. It was reshaped, notched, and named *dientes,* the Spanish word for teeth. This was used to create hair textures and to score (scratch) pieces of clay (such as arms) that need to be attached to clay figures.

Should you want to make your own tools, here are some suggestions:

A. The needle tool is made by embedding a large needle into a piece of ½-inch dowling.

B. Wire tool is made by taping a heavy old-fashioned hair pin into a 4-inch piece of dowling.

C. Teeth *dientes* —use a sharp knife and file to make this handy tool by notching an ice cream stick or wooden tongue depressor.

D. Dental tools are excellent; they have many uses.

Art supply and hobby shops carry small quantities of clay, but large ceramic supply houses offer pugged, de-aired clay in plastic bags of 25 pounds. Clay is perfect for use as it comes out of the bag. If your work is interrupted, cover the clay with polyethylene bags until you are ready to work. (This is the type of plastic bag that comes from the dry cleaners.) When clay is stored, it must be kept airtight to preserve the moisture which keeps the clay pliable. If it is kept *closely wrapped* in polyethylene, it will remain pliable until you return to work.

It is important to learn what you can and cannot do as the clay dries, at which point you can add additional clay, stamp designs, or carve into the surface.

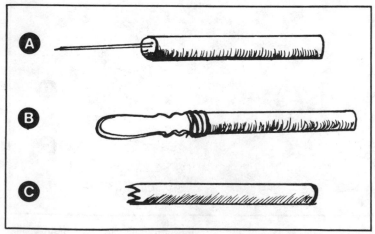

Fig. 2-3. Homemade tools. (A) Needle tool. (B) Wire loop tool. (C) *Dientes* (teeth) tool.

Fig. 2-4. Joann Amparán making "worm" hair on the figure of a centaur in her studio.

CONDITION OF CLAY

When soft and pliable, add arms, legs, tails, decorative buttons, or *worms* of clay (Fig. 2-4). Firmer clay can be combed or textured with a stamp, impressed with a tool or carved with a wire loop or knife.

Squash a wad of soft clay into a small dish, add water, and mix until you have a gooey mixture. This is *slip* or liquid clay, useful as a binder when you join pieces together. Have a clean moist cloth near you as you work, to keep your hands clean.

Keep your working area free from little bits of drying clay. As it collects into small piles, push it under your moist cloth. This gives you freedom to work. It is frustrating to work on a messy surface if you get an idea and need a clear space on which to go promptly to work.

Chapter 3

Playing with Clay

Doing anything creative should give you pleasure, and working with clay can be fun. *Clay* rhymes with *play*, and playing with clay is instinctive to almost anyone who picks it up. Find the person who, given a piece of clay, can resist rolling it about in his hand. Almost unconsciously he will start making a simple form. He may even try to model something. It is a perfectly natural act.

But fun is fun and somewhere along the way there are rules— necessary even for what at first seems like child's play. Without restrictions, you may end up with a mess in your kiln, instead of what you had in mind.

Have fun, but before you start making the interesting pieces shown in this chapter, you must first learn to make a pinch-pot.

MAKING A PINCH-POT

Take a piece of clay large enough to make a ball. Pat the clay between the palms of your hands until it is round and smooth. Holding the ball of clay in your left hand, thrust the thumb of your right hand into the center of the clay. Gently press thumb into clay wall toward the fingers of your right hand, advancing the position of your right hand a little each time.

Repeat this rhythmically, increasing the pressure so that you can feel the wall becoming thinner and the inside hole becoming wider. If you move your thumb and finger position a tiny bit each time, you will make even walls of uniform thickness. Try closing your eyes as you slowly and steadily press your clay. As your piece grows, you can feel the distance between your thumb and fingers and learn to judge the thickness of your walls.

This is good preparation for work at the potter's wheel. The mechanically powered wheel supplies the rotation, but sensitivity to the thickness and contour of the pieces lies in your hands and their control of the clay wall.

BORROWING FROM THE PAST

Primitive pieces suggest ideas which are adaptable to modern decor and fit comfortably into contemporary lifestyles. The concepts and design of ancient pieces are often fascinating, and adaptions from these sources can be equally intriguing. Look for ideas in museums, books on design, magazines, galleries, and exhibits.

This fish container (Fig. 3-1) was inspired by an ancient Mexican clay piece and made by the pinch-pot method. To make this piece you start with a ball of clay and open it from the center (Fig. 3-2). Leave 1½ to 2 inches of clay at the bottom; you will need it later (Fig. 3-3). Press hardest with the lower part of the thumb and fingers to control the opening. Don't let the top flare out too much (Figs. 3-4 and 3-5).

Fig. 3-1. Fish container made by pinch-pot method. An adaptation from ancient Mexican clay piece.

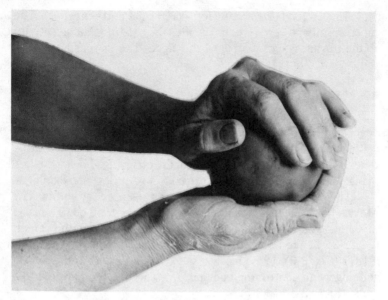

Fig. 3-2. Making a ball out of the clay by rolling and patting it between the palms of your hands.

Fig. 3-3. Hold the ball of clay in your left hand, then push thumb of your right hand into the center of the clay, within an inch and a half (1 ½ inches) of the bottom.

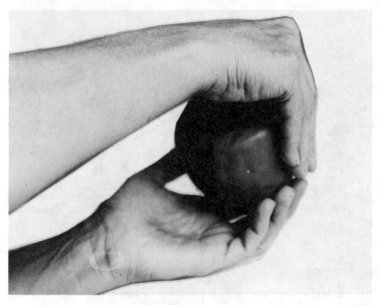

Fig. 3-4. The pressure of the clay between the thumb and the fingers will form the walls of your pot.

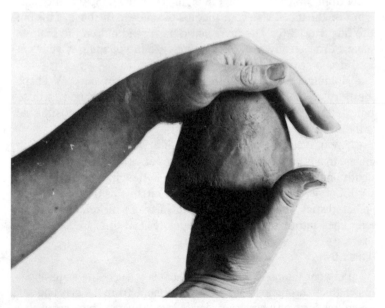

Fig. 3-5. Press very hard with the ends of your thumbs and fingers, so that you do not open the top of the piece too wide.

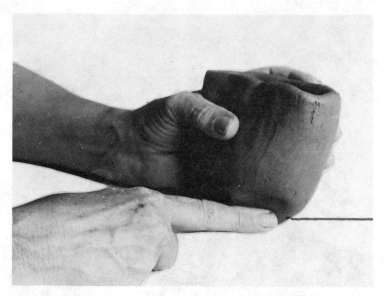

Fig. 3-6. Set the pot firmly on the table to flatten the bottom. Then, with the index finger, press out a fin shape.

When your walls are about ½ inch thick all around (except for the bottom, which should be 1 inch thick or more), tap the thick part firmly on the table. Use your thumbs to squeeze the base of the pot into fins (Fig. 3-6). The fins should be spread out on the table to make a firm, steady base. *Gently* squeeze the opening of your pot until it is an oval shape.

Holding your piece with the left hand, cut out a V shape one-third of the way across the rim of the oval-shaped form to indicate a fish mouth (Fig. 3-7). Repeat this cut on the opposite side of the oval.

Smooth the sharp clay edge with a wooden tool or a damp sponge that is not too wet. With a pointed stick or a pencil, draw the mouth line; from the point of the V cut in the rim, curve it downward. Carve scalloped or scalelike lines on the fins (Fig. 3-8). With a pointed stick, draw a circle about the size of a nickel, and scratch deep lines into it to indicate the eyes (Fig. 3-9).

Thumb Owl

Put your thumb into an oval ball of clay. Make the walls about ¼ inch thick throughout. Remove your thumb from the clay and set the hollow form on a button of clay. Make two small buttons of clay for the eyes and put them on with slip. Add an elongated triangle of

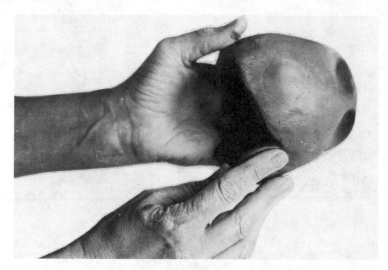

Fig. 3-7. Cut a V-shaped piece of clay to make an open fish-mouth. Smooth the edges with fingers.

clay for a beak between the eyes. Add small triangles of clay for the ears. With steel or modeling tool, add details such as feathers, eyes and feet. Thumb owls are delightful party favors and gifts for collectors (Fig. 3-10, left).

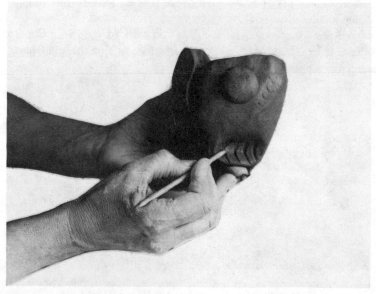

Fig. 3-8. Define the fins by incising sharp lines with the point of a stick.

15

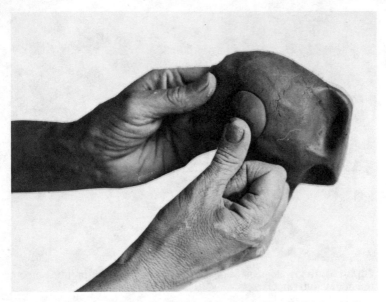

Fig. 3-9. Roll out a marble-sized soft ball of clay and flatten it into a button, then press it into the scored circle.

ANYONE CAN DOODLE!

Fat sausages of clay, buttons, and worms (coils of clay) combine to make clay doodles. All these pieces, made from simple, basic forms, offer endless variety.

Keep a moist cloth near you as you work to keep your fingers clean. Have a bowl of liquid clay nearby for sticking the small parts

Fig. 3-10. Pinch-pot thumb owl at extreme left front of photo. All other pieces were made by rolled out and assembled method.

16

together. Clay can be up to 1 inch thick for these small parts, but they must be *thoroughly* dry before firing.

Clay right out of the bag is perfect for doodling. Sit comfortably at a counter top or table. Work on a smooth surface—wood, Formica, breadboard, or drawing board. Roll out the main piece, the body, first. Figures 3-11 and 3-19 show basic shapes and what they might become—a girl, a boy, a cat.

Press doodle parts firmly together using liquid clay. Where parts are big enough, score the surface with a pointed stick (i.e.,

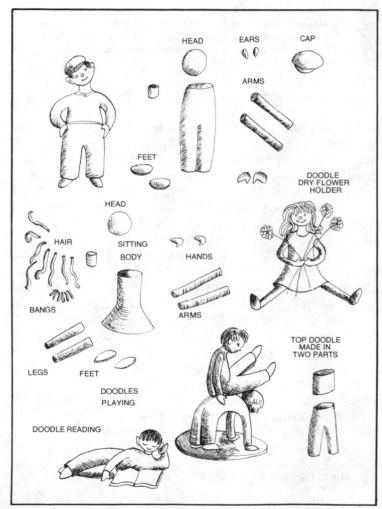

Fig. 3-11. Basic shapes may be combined to form complex figures.

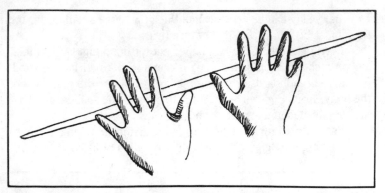

Fig. 3-12. Rolling out worms of clay. Using all your fingers, move them up and down the length of the clay, keeping your fingers flat and not too close together. Don't use the palms of your hands.

arms and legs to body, etc.) Smaller pieces (feet, ears, hands) may be put on using liquid slip only.

Placing doodles in different positions is fun. You can make personalized gifts of your doodles when they are bisque-fired and painted, or glazed for a second firing. Doodle-caricatures of your friends and their activities are welcomed gifts. They also make great party place cards or favors. Golfers, tennis players, and other sports figures are popular. Hats or other costume details that identify a person offer good subjects for doodles. So do anniversaries, weddings, and other special events.

Be sure all doodle parts are *firmly* attached before you leave them to dry, and that the figures are balanced and do not tip over. Pieces can be mounted on a small clay base to insure this. The seated doodle in Fig. 3-11 has enough space between her arms and body to insert a small dry flower bouquet. Also pictured in Fig. 3-11 are two doodles playing leap-frog. The doodle on top is made in two pieces. The moisture of your clay is most important. Always keep the clay that you are not using covered with plastic. Don't try to use clay that has begun to harden the least bit. All your clay parts should be covered as they are made, so that when they are put together, all the clay is of the same consistency. It is essential to know what you can do with clay at different stages of drying.

The Worm Turns to High Fashion

Most anyone picks up a piece of clay for the first time rolls it into a ball or a *worm*, a little coil of clay, as shown in Fig. 3-12.

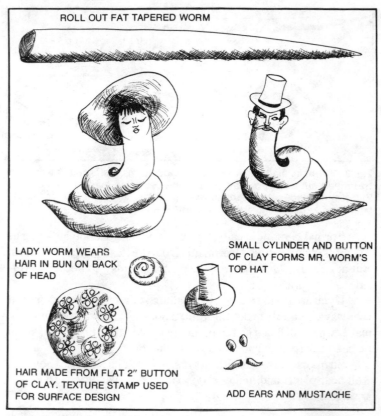

ROLL OUT FAT TAPERED WORM

LADY WORM WEARS
HAIR IN BUN ON BACK
OF HEAD

SMALL CYLINDER AND BUTTON
OF CLAY FORMS MR. WORM'S
TOP HAT

HAIR MADE FROM FLAT 2" BUTTON
OF CLAY. TEXTURE STAMP USED
FOR SURFACE DESIGN

ADD EARS AND MUSTACHE

Fig. 3-13. Worms with style.

Shown here are some worms with style (Fig. 3-13). These stylish worms with their turn-of-the-century hats are conversation pieces.

Roll out finger-width worms, about 10 inches long, tapered to a point on one end. Coil in a circle from the pointed end, letting the fat end stand upright on the coil. Hair, hats, noses, give character to the face.

Another Worm Turns and Becomes a Snail

The snail is a decorative creature, if not appreciated in the garden. To make a clay snail, start with a tapered worm and roll a firm, fat end, leaving a tapered end to trail behind the coil. Set the coil on its side and press down firmly. Spread bottom worm of coil to form a side base so the piece doesn't tip over easily. A second short worm serves as the snail's body emerging from its coiled shell (Fig. 3-14).

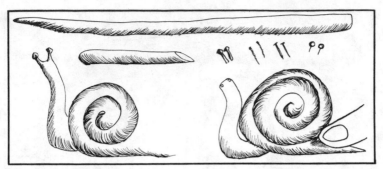

Fig. 3-14. Snails made with two rolled-out worms. Left: snail made from two rolled-out worms of clay; protruding eyes also made from clay. Right: snail made with rolled out worms of clay. Holes are left for eyes, to be inserted after firing. Tacks, wire, etcetera are used.

Formal ceramic techniques would *never* condone anything as flimsy as snail eyes which protrude from the head on slender tubes. But at *Clay In Particular* the desire for whimsy sometimes overrules mere practicality.

If you are daring enough to go along with this theory, there are two ways to do it: make the protrusions as thick as possible, or make two small holes on top of the head and, after firing, add small pieces of wire or wood. Map pins add color.

Snails can be made with worms up to 1½ inch thick. They look well near plants and, being clay, are welcome additions to flower arrangements.

Turtle and Toadstool

This decorative creature is easily assembled. Roll out a long head, neck, and four legs. Flatten a ball of clay for his shell. Make thumbprints on the rim and top of the shell to create a texture. Score the inside of the shell, add slip, and attach ends of neck, legs and tail well into the shell cavity (Fig. 3-15). Turn the form over and check the positions of the legs and head. Add the tail. Draw a mouth line and add eyes, either open or half-closed as shown.

Prop up the long neck until clay is firm. Do not make the head too large, or it will fall forward. The rear legs should be made heavier than the front legs in order to balance the figure.

The important thing in making a toadstool is to maintain the balance. The stem is a fat sausage of clay, which you press down firmly, letting the bottom spread a little to give it a firm base. The top is a ball of clay flattened out in the cup of your hand. Taking a pointed stick, draw fine lines radiating from the center. (Fig. 3-16).

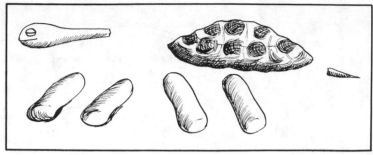

Fig. 3-15. Turtle.

Frog

This frog is humanistic rather than literal. He can be draped in many ways and positions. He can sit, lie on his side or back, or be draped under or over a toadstool. Eyes may be closed or opened. You can mount him on a lily pad, as he may be quite fragile. However you make him, the frog is popular with almost everyone.

Make a pear-shaped body. Cut the round bottom on two sides to form a wedge shape. Score this flat area and add slip before attaching the fat upper part of the frog's leg (Fig. 3-17).

You must decide the position of the body so you will know how to attach the legs. The top of a frog's leg is gently flattened against the scored surface. A frog's leg can be rolled out in the palm of your hand. Leave the top of the leg fat, taper it to thin, and leave a thick part at the end for a webbed foot.

You might have to use a small wad of clay to support the frog when you put him in certain positions (for example, when he is lying on his side supported by his foreleg).

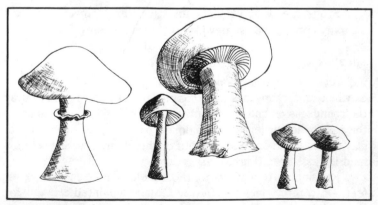

Fig. 3-16. Toadstools.

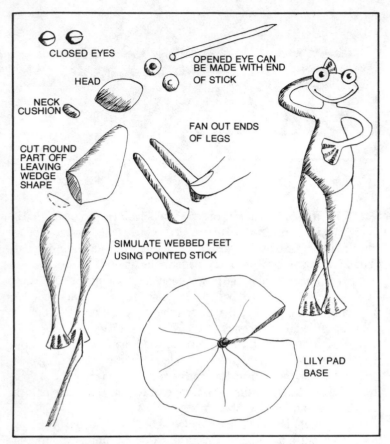

CLOSED EYES

HEAD

OPENED EYE CAN BE MADE WITH END OF STICK

NECK CUSHION

CUT ROUND PART OFF LEAVING WEDGE SHAPE

FAN OUT ENDS OF LEGS

SIMULATE WEBBED FEET USING POINTED STICK

LILY PAD BASE

Fig. 3-17. Making the frog.

Frogs are good subjects for caricature, since the frog's anatomy corresponds somewhat to human anatomy.

Mice

If you feel you have a delicate touch, you might like to make a clay mouse. Start by making a modified pear shape. Then cut away the roundness on both sides of the pear-shaped bottom and score the area for adding legs. In the palm of your hand, roll out a worm of clay that is fat on one end and thin on the other. Shape this into a hind leg as shown (Fig. 3-18).

Roll out two thin worms for the front legs. Flatten the ends for feet. Draw three fine lines for toes. Make a pointed clay egg for head. Make a small ball, flattened out, for a neck. Roll out a long tapered worm for the tail. It might be more practical for a beginner to mount these fragile mice on a small clay base.

First, score the surface you cut from the base of the body and, adding slip, attach the legs. Set this on a clay base, using a wad of clay base to support the body and take the weight off the slim part of legs. This wad should be removed when legs are firm enough to support mouse's body. Add the "arms," head, neck and ears with slip. Affix firmly but gently, using a moist brush to smooth out lines.

The cat (Fig. 3-19), cuddly bear (Fig. 3-20), and elephant (Fig. 3-21) were all made using the same base technique.

Bring on the Clowns!

Clowns can be made from simple clay shapes. Roll out a clay ball for a head, two pear shapes for full-sleeved arms, and a long pear shape for the body and baggy pants. Make two round, flat pieces for the ruffled collar, two smaller ones for the ankles, and

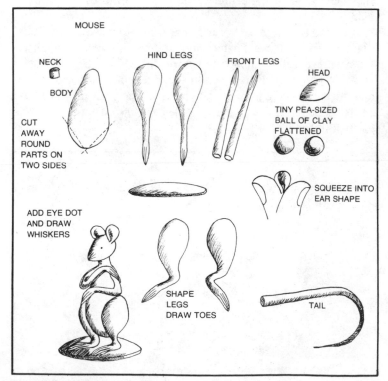

MOUSE

NECK

BODY

HIND LEGS

FRONT LEGS

HEAD

TINY PEA-SIZED BALL OF CLAY FLATTENED

CUT AWAY ROUND PARTS ON TWO SIDES

SQUEEZE INTO EAR SHAPE

ADD EYE DOT AND DRAW WHISKERS

SHAPE LEGS DRAW TOES

TAIL

Fig. 3-18. Making the mouse.

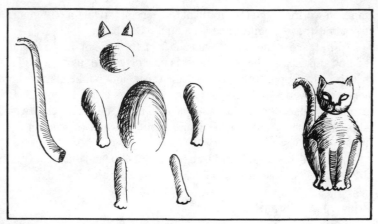

Fig. 3-19. Sitting cat.

two still smaller pieces for the sleeves. These can have lines pressed in, rotating from the center. An old metal lipstick holder cuts a clean hole in the center of the set of six ruffles. (Figs. 3-22, 3-23).

Divide the large part of the pear shape to make baggy pants. Make two oval shapes for feet and, adding slip, place a medium-sized circle of ruffles on top. Add more slip, and set the clown body on ruffles and feet. Firmly attach the sleeved arms to body. You might have to add a prop of clay under the arms to prop them up until they are firmer. The prop should be removed before it begins to stick to the piece.

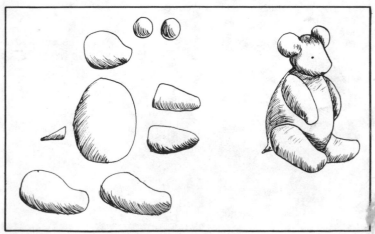

Fig. 3-20. Cuddly bear.

24

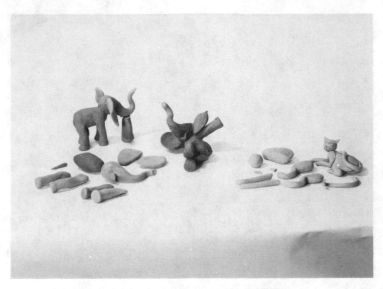

Fig. 3-21. Elephants and cat; simple component shapes used are shown.

Put ruffles on the end of each sleeve with a dab of slip. Make some clown hands. Either shape them like a mitten or roll out a glove-hand as follows: make a round button for palms. Roll out a long, slim clay worm and cut 10 short lengths. Curve two of these pieces outward to make thumbs. Firmly add the fingers to round clay buttons. These hands are stuck to the small ruffle button with slip.

Fig. 3-22. When all these little clay parts are made, they are assembled to complete the clown figure shown at right of photo.

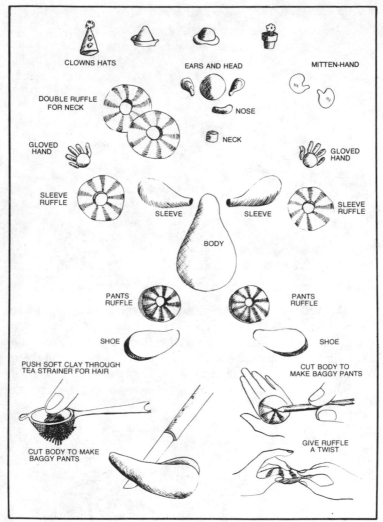

Fig. 3-23. Components of the clown.

You can make your clown expressive by the position of the hands and arms. Give a twist to the double collar, pants, and neck ruffles. Stick on the neck, head, ears, nose, hair and hat. Hair can be made with soft clay pushed through a tea strainer or sieve.

Apply a drop of slip on face in front of the ear and in a line around the base of head. Add some hair carefully and press on to a trail of slip. Leave the top of the head bare. The clown looks good with or without a hat, or with a flower pot on top.

Find a good place to dry your clown. Set the clown on a piece of paper. Press the feet firmly, making sure he is balanced. Leave the figure to dry. After he is *thoroughly* dry, he is ready for bisque-firing. If kiln-firing is a problem, paint him with bright acrylic colors or watercolor. Or he can be decorated with under-glaze, then glazed and fired again. Low-fire clay and Cone 04 to 06 firing is well suited to these smaller items.

Chapter 4

Designing
with Clay Ribbons

Ribbons! The word suggests motion, rhythm, grace. To Joann Amparán, it suggested a new way to create smart-looking containers. To make her basket-containers she uses ribbons of clay. The shapes of her ribbon baskets are varied: rectangular, round and oval, without or with decoration.

They are designed to hang or to be used for planting. They are interesting pieces for still-life groupings, or, using a solid container inside the basket, pieces in which to work out unusual floral arrangements.

The baskets take on an entirely different character when they float in space. Swing them from a metal hanger which you can find at a local nursery or hardware store. Place the baskets in a macrame sling for an exotic touch.

All of the baskets shown in this book were made upside-down, draped over a mold or form of some sort. At *Clay In Particular*, Benigno threw a deep, simple bowl with a rounded bottom. This served as a perfect drape-mold. This was bisque-fired. The advantage of the bisque-fired form is that you can drape your clay ribbons directly over this absorbent surface. When clay ribbons become firm, the piece may be easily removed from the bisque mold.

The basket shown in Fig. 4-1 was made over an inverted plastic bowl covered with a polyethylene bag. The bag is necessary to separate your clay ribbons from sticking to the mold-form, if it is anything other than a bisque mold-form. When you make your basket, use at least four layers of this soft plastic.

28

MATERIALS NEEDED FOR THE RIBBON BASKET

To make your ribbon basket you will need:

- ☐ A flat surface such as a kitchen counter, table, or drawing board; a breadboard, no smaller than 12 inches by 16 inches, might do.
- ☐ A piece of heavy cloth; preferably canvas or duck.
- ☐ A mixing bowl without a rim or spout.
- ☐ Wooden paddle.
- ☐ A long knife, fettling knife, or wooden tool with a good cutting edge.
- ☐ Bowl for water.
- ☐ Sponge: Mediterranean, or elephant ear. A fine synthetic or bath sponge (cut in half) will do.
- ☐ Polyethylene bags (from dry cleaners).
- ☐ A yardstick, preferably aluminum.
- ☐ Lazy Susan, banding wheel or turn-table (optional).
- ☐ Plaster or wooden bat, piece of board or Masonite, 12 to 14 inches.
- ☐ Two ¼-inch sticks at least 16 inches in length. For larger pieces, sticks will be thicker and longer.

Fig. 4-1. The completed, unfired ribbon basket pictured in a series of step-by-step photos in this chapter.

☐ A rolling pin, thick piece of dowling, or a length of pipe.
☐ Clay.

You might have some clay from school, community, or hobby shop projects. Chances are it is a low-firing clay body (Cone 04 to Cone 06). If you want to use this clay, you might add sand or *grog*, a finely ground, fired clay which you can buy at ceramics supply houses. But the directions for making these baskets apply only to stoneware clay that fires to Cone 10. Ribbons cut from this clay are flexible and drape easily over the form.

Cone 10 porcelain makes lovely smaller baskets or soap dishes. Porcelain, without sand or grog added, has a tendency to crack, especially if you try to stretch it over a large area. Small pieces, however, made with porcelain ribbons (¼ inch by ¼ inch), are lacy and elegant, especially when glazed and fired in a C/10 reduction kiln.

If you own commercial slab-making equipment, the ribbon-making process is greatly simplified. If you don't have a slab-maker, proceed as follows:

STARTING THE RIBBON BASKET

Start your basket by rolling out a piece of clay ½ inch thick (Fig. 4-2). Use a bowl or jar to cut a pancake of clay large enough to make a solid bottom for your basket.

Start with half a bag of clay—12½ pounds. Roll the clay out on a canvas surface between two sticks. Place a yardstick at the outer edges of the rolled-out clay and press firmly as you cut the clay ribbons the full length of the clay (Fig. 4-3).

Move the yardstick over one width to cut your next ribbon (Fig. 4-4). Repeat the process until you have cut as many ribbons as possible.

Carefully unpeel the first ribbon (Fig. 4-5) and lay it on another surface where the sharp edges may be softened with a sponge. Repeat this until you have sponged six ribbons and have them flexible and ready to use (Fig. 4-6).

Turn your mold-form over on the bat or board. Cover with the plastic bag, tucking it under securely, and taping it down if necessary. Press your pancake of clay on the mold-form. Take one ribbon in both hands. Press one end of the ribbon firmly onto the pancake, which is now the *bottom* of your basket. This takes about 1½ inches of your ribbon. Allow the ribbon to fall easily into a loop (Fig. 4-7) over the side of your mold-form. Bring it back and press it firmly over the ribbon at its starting point.

Fig. 4-2. Rolling out pancake of clay for bottom of basket.

Fig. 4-3. Starting to cut clay ribbons using a yardstick.

Fig. 4-4. Cutting second ribbon, the full length of the clay.

On the opposite side of your mold-form, make another loop and cut it (Figs. 4-8 and 4-9). After you have placed the second

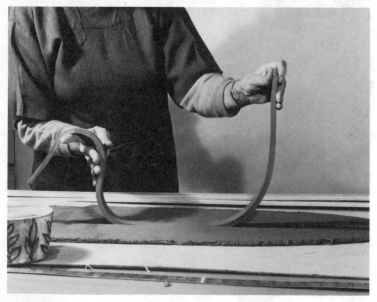

Fig. 4-5. Unpeeling the cut ribbon.

Fig. 4-6. Softening sharp edges with sponge.

Fig. 4-7. Allowing ribbon to fall easily into a loop.

Fig. 4-8. Making second loop on opposite side of mold-form.

loop, fill in with two more loops on either side. Make certain that the ends of all the loops are attached firmly to the bottom.

A fettling knife is good for cutting the ribbons as you press them down (Fig. 4-10). If you are using a turntable, revolve it slowly with one hand while gradually paddling the loops onto the base (Fig. 4-11).

THE SECOND ROW OF LOOPS

You are now ready to make a second row of loops. These loops are shorter than those of the first group. Use the same procedure, placing the smaller loops on top of the larger loops (Fig. 4-12). Gently pat the row of loops. Be careful not to squash the ribbons out of shape (Fig. 4-13).

Using the palm, or your paddle, exert pressure to force the ribbons together without squashing them. This gradual pressure binds the pieces together and make a strong, sturdy basket. If the basket is *too* open, it is not practical (Fig. 4-14).

TEXTURING THE RIBBONS

Texture stamps may be used on the bottom or any part of the basket. Round balls of clay, pressed firmly onto the places where

Fig. 4-9. Cutting end of ribbon.

Fig. 4-10. Pressing and cutting ribbons with fettling knife.

35

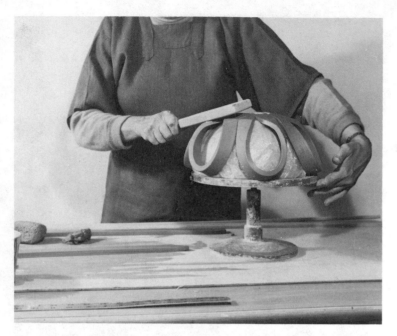

Fig. 4-11. Paddling loops onto the base.

Fig. 4-12. Placing smaller loops on top of larger loops.

Fig. 4-13. Gently pat loops with your fingers to keep ribbons from squashing.

Fig. 4-14. Paddling ribbons together.

Fig. 4-15. Adding balls of clay for texturing.

the ribbons overlap (Fig. 4-15), add interest to your surface design and lend strength to the piece (Fig. 4-16).

Allow the basket to become firm enough so that the mold can be turned over without the loops drooping or flopping. Use a spatula or flat knife to lift the mold-form and basket. Place the board on top, turning both mold and basket over on flat surface, to first remove the mold-form from inside the basket. Next, *gently* pull away the plastic covering, adding clay to fill any holes, openings, or gaps. Put it in a safe dry place and cover it lightly, so that it will dry evenly.

BASKETS FROM CIRCLES OF CLAY

Figures 4-17 through 4-19 show baskets made from ribbons that were complete circles. These were cut from a cylinder thrown on the wheel. The ribbons were cut while the wheel was turning slowly. A needle-tool was inserted about 1 inch from the top while the wheel made a complete turn. A knife such as the one described in Chapter 7 could be used. The wheel was then stopped and the ring of clay gently lifted off and laid on a board (Fig. 4-20).

If you are going to produce a number of these baskets, this is the best method. At one time the baskets were produced in quantity, but this proved impractical because of the shipping. The closely overlapped continuous loops make a sturdy basket, as there is no need to cut or piece parts together. This also tends to make a heavier piece, better suited as a planter or standing pot rather than a hanging basket. Ribbons were pinched together to make a strong, dramatic footing.

See also Figs. 4-21 through 4-24.

The Soap or Candy Dish

Bowls, boxes, or woven baskets covered with plastic can be used as mold-forms to drape small ribbons on when making these

Fig. 4-16. Texturing the bottom of the basket.

Fig. 4-17. Rectangular standing pot made from circles of clay. Clay bands reinforce sides of this tall 10-inch-by-11-inch planter which holds a nursery gallon plant.

useful, smaller items. However, plaster molds are best of all, as they needn't be covered with plastic. The plaster surface is porous and absorbs the clay's moisture until piece naturally pulls away from the mold-form. Round, square, and oval mold-forms, shown in

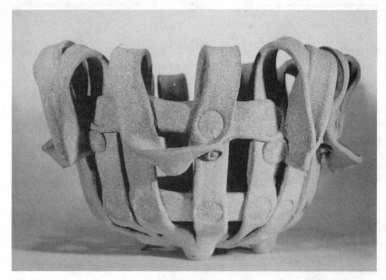

Fig. 4-18. This pot has an inside strap of clay. Long loops were draped back over an added outside strap of clay. Texture stamps reinforced the connecting points.

Fig. 4-19. This tall basket was made from circles of clay. Each loop was made from a continuous circle of clay. One circle was pinched together in four places to form a design and strengthen the piece.

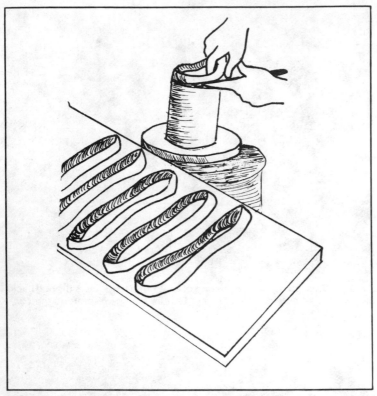

Fig. 4-20. Cutting the clay ribbons off the cylinder.

(Fig. 4-25), were made by pouring casting plaster into Styrofoam fast-food hamburger and sandwich containers.

After you have placed your mold-form on a bat or board, cut clay ribbons as shown in ribbon basket sequences. These ribbons needn't be over 12 to 14 inches long. Divide ribbon into 3/16-, ¼-, or ½-inch widths. Cut these into shorter pieces as needed for your design.

Sponge the ribbons lightly to make them smooth and pliable before shaping them into spiral loops, etc. Begin your piece by draping ribbons across and around base of the mold-form. This makes a basic frame within which you add swirls (Fig. 4-26), loops, and balls of clay pressed firmly with a texture stamp. If you are making a soap dish, pierce a few holes in the bottom for drainage (unless, of course, it is an open design).

If the pattern of your ribbon is widely spaced, drilling separate holes isn't necessary. Remember that these small ribbons must overlap and be firmly pressed together. If not, as they firm up in drying, they will break apart. Balls of clay make feet for the piece. Squeeze clay into a small pyramid and affix to the bottom with slip; press or paddle on firmly. When the clay feels firm (*not* dried out!), turn the mold and piece over, pressing down on the mold-form until the piece is balanced and doesn't tip to one side. When the clay is firm to the touch, press the edge of the frame all around to see if it separates easily from the mold. If it resists, leave it to set up for another half-hour or hour. (This depends entirely upon the dryness of the air. *Never* leave a piece at this stage without covering it, as

Fig. 4-21. A group of ribbon baskets of various shapes, sizes and techniques by Joann Amparán.

Fig. 4-22. Delicate dry flower arrangement is perfect complement to the flowing lines of Joann's handsome double-loop ribbon basket, enhanced further by texture stamp designs.

you might forget it and find it cracked off the mold when you return.)

All the ribbon baskets shown in this chapter, including those in Fig. 4-27, were fired to Cone 10 in a reduction atmosphere without any glaze or stain.

A Ribbon Flower Vase

Here is a good way to make a lovely, lacy sheath to disguise a plain glass and complement your bouquet.

Find a tall pint jar or tumbler to use as a mold-form. Cover it with plastic and tape firmly with masking or cellophane tape. Roll out a small circle of clay and place on top of your mold-form. Make ribbons no wider than ½ inch. Attach the tops of the loops to your clay circle. Secure the first series of loops. You can try making two rows of loops or long loops in a figure-8, placed close together (Fig. 4-28).

These are just two suggested designs; you will think of many more. Straps of clay around the form are necessary if you want your vertical loops to be open and lacy. Follow same procedure as described in the step-by-step series on the ribbon basket in this chapter.

44

These smaller pieces make unusual and original gifts; one idea will lead to another. Low-fired clay bodies (Cone 04 to Cone 06) are well suited to these smaller ribbon pieces. They are easily glazed. Where you have solid areas of clay, they can be decorated with underglaze colors or transparent glazes. A transparent mat is particularly attractive on open pieces. Figure 4-29 shows a soap

Fig. 4-23. This clay basket was made over a round wastebasket. This basket is large enough for the 1 gallon plant containers used at commercial nurseries.

Fig. 4-24. Group of stoneware ribbon baskets by Joann Amparan.

dish made with surface decoration. The group of soap dishes (Fig. 4-30) were all made with Cone 10 porcelain clay, but could be made with a white, low-fire clay. An immense range of Cone 06 glazes are available; you can match your colors to the decor of any room.

CLAY RIBBON HAIR: AN ART DECO FLAIR

If you are clever at modeling heads, you might want to test your originality by adding clay ribbon hair. The nature of the ribbons encourages serendipity. Being flexible, they are easily coaxed into curls, loose waves, or flying strands from which you create your own exotic hair style.

Study each face in Figs. 4-31 through 4-34. Observe how the hair style complements the features and the position of the head.

If it helps in deciding the style you want, make a few rough sketches. Will a small cluster of heavy ribbons be better than a large number of small ribbons? Do you want to use bangs? Ideas will come spontaneously as you work and do a little experimenting.

In Fig. 4-31, the neck of the 8″ head was thrown on the wheel. The head, as wheel-thrown, began as an egg-shape. The features were modeled by pushing from the inside while adding clay chin and nose on the outside. When the modeling was completed, the two pieces were joined with slip.

Starting at the crown, 3-inch clay ribbons were combed, flattened at the ends so they would fall gracefully, and arranged around the face. The extravagant loops were flattering to the piquant features. Stained with redwood, the hair acquired a rich terra cotta tone when fired at Cone 10 in reduction.

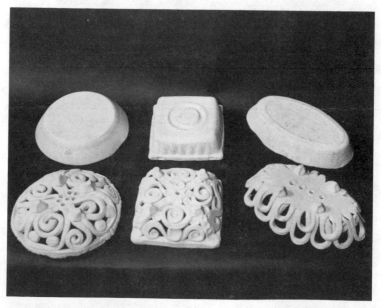

Fig. 4-25. Round, square and oval mold-forms were made from fast-food containers. Lower line: Ribbon pieces made from mold-forms (shown above) after being bisque-fired.

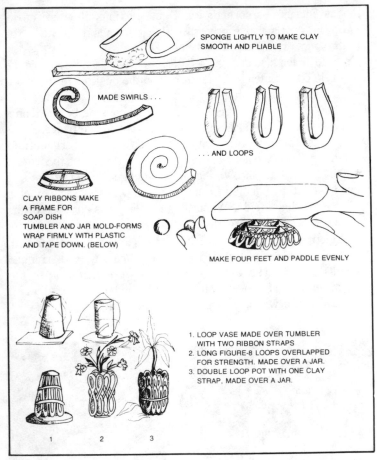

SPONGE LIGHTLY TO MAKE CLAY SMOOTH AND PLIABLE

MADE SWIRLS . . .

. . . AND LOOPS

CLAY RIBBONS MAKE
A FRAME FOR
SOAP DISH
TUMBLER AND JAR MOLD-FORMS
WRAP FIRMLY WITH PLASTIC
AND TAPE DOWN. (BELOW)

MAKE FOUR FEET AND PADDLE EVENLY

1. LOOP VASE MADE OVER TUMBLER
   WITH TWO RIBBON STRAPS
2. LONG FIGURE-8 LOOPS OVERLAPPED
   FOR STRENGTH. MADE OVER A JAR.
3. DOUBLE LOOP POT WITH ONE CLAY
   STRAP, MADE OVER A JAR.

1   2   3

Fig. 4-26. Working with clay ribbons.

The modeled, sophisticated face in Fig. 4-32 was placed on a board. Starting at the crown, clay ribbons were shifted about, and squeezed together in places. At certain points, slip was added, ribbons were scored and pinched together. When completed, the piece was laid out on a kiln slab and fired at Cone 10 reduction. Iron oxide was applied heavily so the piece has a metallic finish.

Only a head whose modeling is as sensitive as that in Fig. 4-33 can effectively use such a curly coiffure. The eyes were cut out from the clay with a needle tool. This piece is unfired.

If you are a novice at modeling, it would be best to try a less difficult face, one with bold, simple features. There are many examples of faces falling into this category in this book. Chapter

11, *Dama de la Olla*, for example, shows step-by-step pictures and gives direction for uncomplicated modeling.

Try it, you might like it!

GENERAL TIPS ON MAKING CLAY BASKETS

Once you understand the basic techniques, the way you make your basket is up to you. The shape and size of the basket depends on the shape and size of what you use as a mold-form. Regardless of your preference, you can usually find something comparable in a plastic container at a supermarket or hardware store. Make sure the container has no feet, spouts or handles.

You must not leave large gaps between the ribbons *if your basket is to be over 10 inches deep*. If, as you press the loops one over another, you find weak or thin areas, you can add clay buttons. Press them firmly over the weak spots, and texture the clay with a stamp.

If you wish to make a basket that is open and lacy, you will need to add at least one strap of clay around the center of the basket. *Two* would be even better.

Suppose you are going to make a large planter to hold a gallon-size plant. Start with a plastic wastebasket, approximately 7 inches wide and 11 inches deep. This is your mold-form. When using large plastic containers as mold-forms, use masking or cellophane tape to make the polyethylene stay snugly in place. It

Fig. 4-27. Shown here are three pieces made from mold-forms, right side up. Square soap dish at upper left was glazed with waxy white. Soap dish at lower center glazed with brown Temoku.

Fig. 4-28. Narrow ribbon basket made over a glass jar.

should not hang loosely around the mold-form or stick out between the ribbons. Let it cling as closely to the mold-form as possible.

If you want a strong, dramatic, or sculptural piece, use thick ribbons. Drape the ribbon loops so that they lap over one another, and you won't have to use clay straps. Using thick ribbons, you will be able to make loops, scrolls, curls, plumes and the like. Because the clay *is* thick you can really 'sculpt' the basket by pressing, pushing and smoothing the clay.

Plastic wastebaskets, tubs, and bowls are excellent for making large planters. Always cover the form used as a mold with

Fig. 4-29. Porcelain ribbon loops are brought together to form the bottom of this soap dish. Leaf and flower design in blue and green brushed on with underglaze.

Fig. 4-30. Sixteen variations of soap dishes made with clay ribbon technique. Oval, square, and rectangular shapes were all made over plaster mold-forms, from porcelain clay.

51

Fig. 4-31. Piquant face is framed with combed clay ribbon hair style, spectacular loops. Redwood stain produces a rich terra cotta color on hair; 8 inches tall.

plastic. The drying of the basket is determined by the atmosphere of the room. The basket might dry in an hour, or it might take overnight. Depending on the dryness of the air, it could be kept indefinitely. A basket left too long, however, will dry out and crack. Experience, once again, is your best teacher.

Once you have made this basic basket, you will realize that the ribbon lengths, thickness of the clay and size of the form you are using to drape your ribbons are variable factors. Unless you are going to produce a commercial line, you will probably make a different piece each time. The possibilities are endless.

For a remake of the film *Lost Horizons, Clay In Particular* was commissioned to make fifteen baskets 16 inch by 18 inch in size. Each basket held a fat candle and was placed in a huge sling that ended in an enormous colorful tassel. Spread throughout the scenes of Shangri-la, they looked spectacular.

Keep hanging baskets as light as possible, but seal them well at the connecting points. Make the piece stronger by adding clay straps near the top and bottom. You will notice how straps are used in many of the ribbon baskets shown in this chapter.

These stoneware baskets are fragile, despite their sturdy appearance, even fired to Cone 10. Those produced over plastic wastebaskets were made from clay ribbons ½ inch thick, and many buttons of clay were pressed into the surface with texture stamps.

These baskets will be heavy and should be placed away from areas where there is a lot of foot traffic. They show off best in

Fig. 4-32. Streaming strands of clay ribbon hair around the face of an Art Deco head. Iron oxide, applied heavily, gave it a metallic finish. Wall piece is 10 inches high.

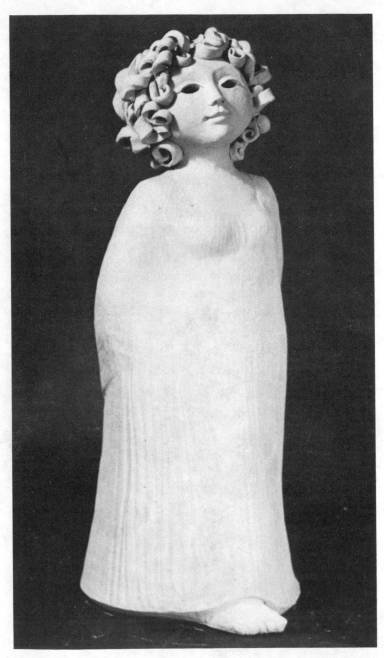

Fig. 4-33. Elaborate clay ribbon hair style surrounds the sensitive face on this figure modeled by Joann. Eyes were cut out with a needle tool.

Fig. 4-34. Clay ribbons 1 inch wide fall in graceful loops around the delicately modeled face of this art nouveau head. Texture stamp designs on high collar. Clay worms made to create lacy ruffles around the neckline. Mounted on a stained walnut base.

dramatic settings. As long as they are made with extended loops and protruding edges they must be treated like fine European China. Their rugged appearance belies their fragility.

If there is a chance that your basket is drying too fast, because of the weather or atmospheric conditions, cover it with plastic. Drying can be hurried by using an electric fan, turning the piece often so that the basket dries evenly.

Chapter 5

Embellishing the Clay Surface

When you have finished making a piece, whether it is thrown, or made with a slab or coil method, you may want to embellish the surface.

TEXTURE STAMPS

As a start, you might try texture stamps. You have already discovered ways in which they can be used effectively. You have also learned that they offer one of the simplest and most direct ways to decorate clay (Fig. 5-1). Clay stamps should be made ahead of time to allow for drying and bisque-firing. The bisque-fire gives you a permanent tool.

A rich surface decoration may be obtained by the use of texture stamps. Make them by rolling out a 2 inch-by-3 inch cone of clay, flatten one of the ends to the size of a quarter, dime, or nickel. Texture stamps may be made any size, but for smaller pieces, these are the most practical.

The illustrations shown include a flowing pattern of wavy lines, made with the sharp point of a manicure stick; lines radiating from the center of the stamp, incised with a knife, and an overall pattern of dots made with the point of a pencil (Fig. 5-2). A planned design can be carved ⅛ inch deep. Tamp the other end of the cone and carve a second design.

Texture stamps are used for adding designs to the costumes of figures: at the neckline, at the bottom of a skirt, or as an overall pattern. When using them near the rim of a pot where the clay is thinner, put your hands *inside the pot* to support as you press the stamp into the clay. If the opening is too small for your hand, insert a round stick to support the pressure when stamping the outside. Stamp directly on the surface, or add a button of clay to the piece, then stamp.

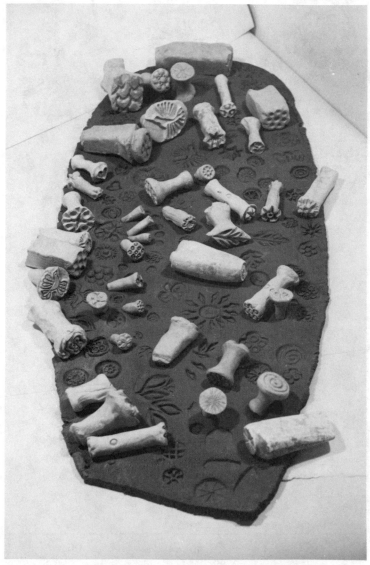

Fig. 5-1. Photo of actual texture stamps used on pieces shown throughout this book.

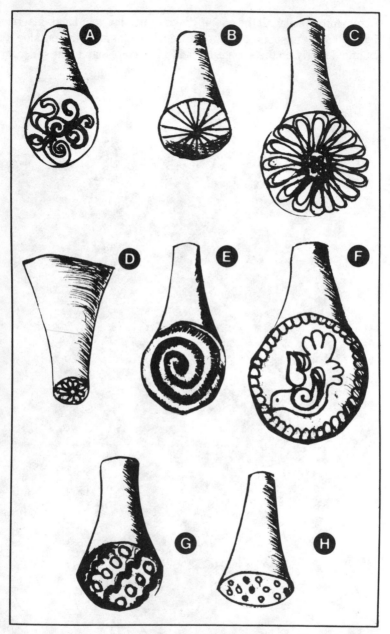

Fig. 5-2. Examples of texture stamps. (A) Wavy lines. (B) Radial lines. (C) Shaggy daisy pattern. (D) Small daisy design. (E) Spiral design. (F) Mexican bird motif, beaded edge. (G) Wavy lines with dots. (H) Dots made with pencil point.

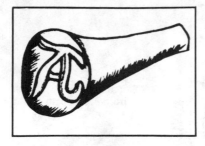

Fig. 5-3. A ⅛-inch relief logo design carved as texture stamp.

You can make a logo of your name or initials to stamp on the bottom of your piece, and so identify your work. The letters will be reversed, so first draw them on clear tracing paper. Then turn the paper over and trace the letters on your stamp before carving them. (Figs. 5-3, 5-4).

Remember that the design you cut into your texture stamp will form the high point on your stamped impression.

The condition of the clay and the pressure exerted will determine the depth or shallowness. Always try out your stamp on a small piece of clay. Play around with the stamps. Have fun experimenting until you arrive at a concept you really like. Then tackle the larger pieces.

For texturing larger pieces such as lamp bases and planters, the rough, porous surface of fire brick is excellent. It can be carved with a sharp knife scoring deep lines, holes and hollows to create a feeling of depth. Figures 5-5 through 5-7 show three designs which were cut into fire brick with a knife, bold patterns in low relief.

Fig. 5-4. Humming bird design on texture stamp. Stamp was used as a logo to identify a Joann ribbon basket.

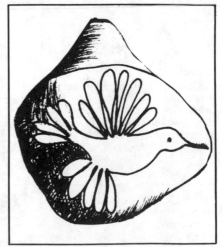

Fig. 5-5. Square flower motif was dug out of porous segment of fire brick with a strong, sharp knife.

With the simplest of forms, circles, triangles, and cube shapes, you will be able to produce an endless variety of patterns which you may use in any way you wish.

Nature is extremely generous in yielding a great many objects for texturing clay. Search for rocks with unusual shapes, tree bark, twigs, and seeds. With a peach stone you can create a rich over-all texture. Don't be afraid to experiment! If you've had no previous experience, it might be well to practice on cast-off pieces of clay until you have what you want, then tackle the large object. Once you start you may be surprised at your own inventiveness! (Figs. 5-8 through 5-11.)

Fig. 5-6. This rectangular design was made from a fragment of fire brick, grooved out and cut with a drill. It was effective when used on the sides of large planters.

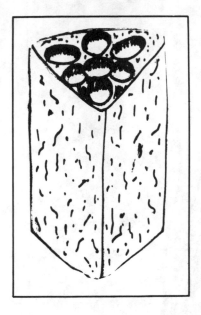

Fig. 5-7. This seven petal design was cut into a rough, porous piece of fire brick with a heavy, pointed knife. The holes might also be made by spinning the ends of a drill to make your pattern.

If you are familiar with plaster of paris and enjoy working with it, you may achieve fine detail by carving into the surface with a sharp pointed knife.

CARVING

Making stripes on shirts, pants, and gowns of clay figures with a wire loop tool leads to more elaborate carving. Incising of the

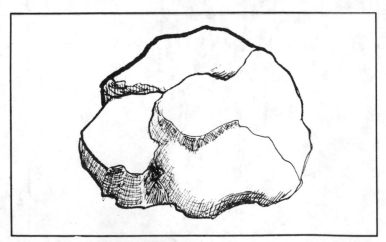

Fig. 5-8. The craggy surface of rocks.

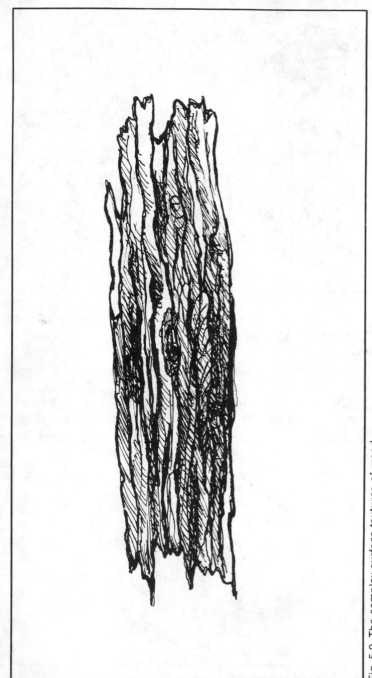

Fig. 5-9. The complex surface textures of wood.

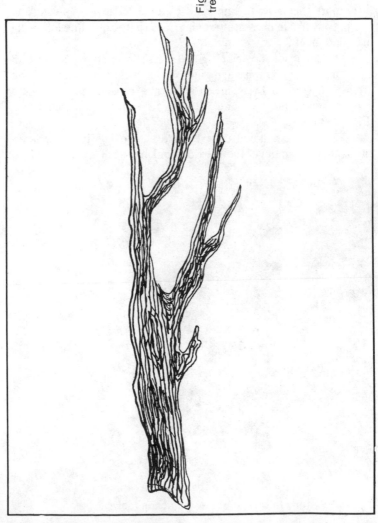

Fig. 5-10. The varying textures of a tree branch.

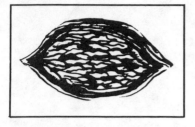

Fig. 5-11. A peach stone makes an especially good texturing tool for creating overall patterns, and is effective for creating fur textures on animal forms.

surface lends interest to pieces that are to be glazed, while deep carving creates a sculptured surface handsome enough to need little more than a light stain. The Kemper R2 proved strong and sharp, easy to use in creating spontaneous patterns while following the contour of a pot.

The small pot shown in Fig. 5-12 has flower center made with a texture stamp. The basic design was incised lightly around the entire pot (Fig. 5-13). The second time around, the tool cuts deeper, and at a sharper angle, to create a bold, dramatic surface (Fig. 5-14).

The double-handled covered urn shown in Fig. 5-25 is an outstanding example of the Mexican influence in clay design. It is

Fig. 5-12. Starting to carve a pot with a ribbon tool.

Fig. 5-13. Basic design was incised lightly around the entire pot.

Fig. 5-14. The design becomes bolder the second time around, as the tool cuts deeper into clay.

Fig. 5-15. Ceramic container to be mounted on the wall for dried or fresh flowers and leaves, or as purely as an ornament. Starting as a sphere open on top, it was flattened on one side for wall mounting. Two holes were made on the back for this purpose. Modeled and incised stylized design creates effective low relief. Stained with red iron oxide. C/10 reduction firing.

both bold and elegant, primitive and sophisticated. Here we find the sun motif surrounded by flamelike rays. Bands of clay are also carved, adding to the richness of the overall pattern. It was stained with iron oxide and reduction firing produced a patina on the raised portions of the entire piece.

WALL POCKETS

Wall pockets to be used as receptacles for weeds, dry flowers, or plants, especially those with trailing foliage, are extremely attractive and easy to produce. The two pieces shown in Figs. 5-15 and 5-16 began as wheel-thrown spheres. Pressed flat on one side, they provided an excellent surface for carving on the other, rounded side.

Enriching and embellishing clay pieces can include modeling and sculpture. Modeled faces create interest in Fig. 5-17 and 5-18. The girl on the rectangular slab-made wall pocket was modeled on a plaster bat, then attached to the carved panel on the front of the clay piece.

Another Modeled Face

The fish-shaped soap container began as a fat clay bottle with a flared top, thrown on the wheel. The first step was to close up the flared top in order to make a wavy fish tail. An amusing jester's face was then modeled on the rounded end of the bottle shape. Large oval openings were cut on both sides. Pointed cones of clay were added to the head and chin for a fool's cap. Small balls of clay were

Fig. 5-16. Clay sphere, open on top, was flattened on one side for wall mounting. Two holes were made on the back for that purpose. Modeled head and incised hair design. Stained with red iron oxide. C/10 reduction firing. May be used purely as decoration or can be effective as a container for fresh flowers, dried flowers and leaves.

Fig. 5-17. Stoneware wall pocket 12 inches tall. Design cut out of clay ¾ inches deep. Figure placed inside pocket allows space for fresh leaves or dried plants.

attached to the ends. The modeled face and bottom were painted with wax resist and the entire piece dipped in waxy white glaze. When dry, accents of yellow, green, blue and brown were added.

You can create a simple pattern with texture stamps. But you can also be more elaborate with carving and modeling—the quality of lush ferns, for example, is harmonious with luxurious surface decoration.

Two examples of carved decoration are seen in the wall pots pictures here. Holes were made on the flat surface for hanging the pieces on interior or exterior walls.

ADDING SOFT CLAY TO THE SURFACE

To make these angel bell/candle holders (Fig. 5-19) with ruffled dresses of *moja* (slip), you start by throwing a cone of clay with a narrow tapered neck. Make the head by throwing a tiny sphere with a deep rim for a crown, allowing enough clay to make a little neck.

The slip accumulates at the bottom of the bowl, or bucket, of water where the potter wets his hands while making clay pieces on

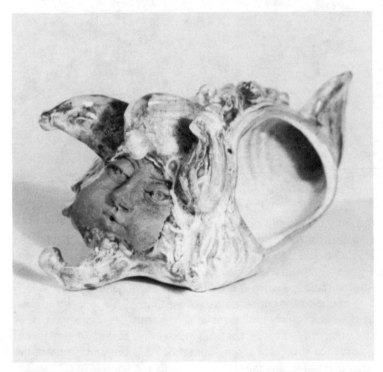

Fig. 5-18. Gonzalo's *Jester of the Sea*, a thrown piece with face and fool's cap added. Waxy white decorated in four colors that fired satisfactorily at Cone 10 reduction.

Fig. 5-19. Angel Bell and Candle Holder. Waxy white glaze; 10″ high. Small angel has *badajo* (clanger) inside. Both angles are designed to hold a candle in the crown. Small angel is 7 inches tall.

the wheel. This slip can be dried out on plaster bats, or stand in a bucket to thicken over a period of time. This is the moja that is used for the angel's gown.

Stir this slip with a *batidor* (a beater or blender) until smooth. After surface moisture is gone from the angel cone, apply a ¼ inch coat of slip to the entire surface of the cone shape. Place the cone on the banding wheel and make a line with the end of a stick or modeling tool through the slip the entire height of the piece. Confidence will come through practice. It is the uniformity of the lines that make this pattern so attractive.

Make a second line (from bottom to top or vice versa) about 1 inch away from the first line. Move the wheel slowly as you add

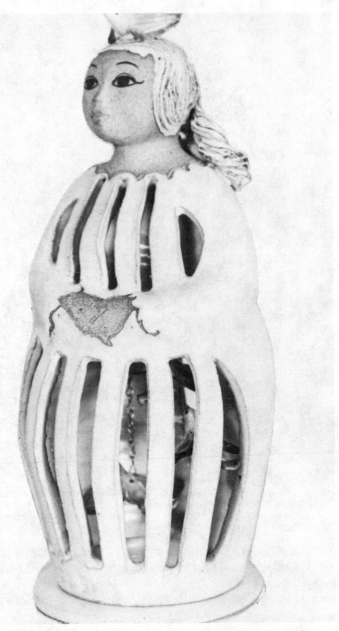

Fig. 5-20. The *pajarera*, bird cage lady, is a thrown piece with cut out design. Dipped in waxy white, decorated detail in underglaze. Tiny bird cage and birds swing inside the peek-through form on a small wire chain. May be removed and replaced by candle, placed in rim on floor of form. 14 inches tall.

Fig. 5-21. Nun votive candle holders, 10 inches and 5 inches tall. A partially covered face is lighted by a candle placed inside the figure on a separate rimmed base. Holes are pierced in the front of the figure, simulating a rosary. Bronze glaze.

lines. Be sure your stick is going deep enough through the slip to touch the clay surface of the cone. Lines will converge toward the neck of the cone and diverge at the bottom. Allow slip to set up somewhat and lose its wet look before scoring top and adding the head.

Nose and mouth can be added to the head while you wait for the slip to dry a little. Make a small donut of clay for the chignon. Comb hair and chignon with the *dientes* tool. Two holes for eyes can be made with a stick. Score the base and neck and add slip before

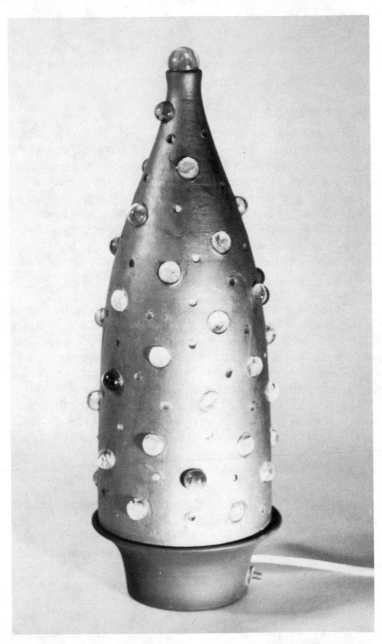

Fig. 5-22. Festive cone-shaped lamp, marbles inserted in holes made with lipstick tubes used as cutters. Separate clay base. Piece can be glazed, but in this instance it was sprayed with gold metallic paint for special occasion.

securing the angel's crowned head on the body. Wings are made from a rolled-out cone shape of clay, pressed flat. This can be decorated with a texture stamp. The angel wings can be added just below the chignon, about an inch apart. Press them firmly into the soft slip surface.

CUT-OUT SURFACES

The *pajarera* or bird cage lady (Fig. 5-20) was made from a wheel-thrown figure like the one detailed in Chapter 11. A separate base was thrown with a rim inside. When the clay became firm, a small wad of clay was pressed into the area where the shoulders begin. Arms were pushed out from the inside. Simple outlines of crossed hands, sleeve and neckline scallops were incised into the figure with a *dientes* tool. When the clay figure was firmer, eleven half-inch vertical openings were cut in the blouse and shirt areas. Four small birds were modeled. One was mounted on top of her head; the other three had a hole made through their bodies and left to dry.

After bisque firing, eyes were painted and wax resist applied to face, neck and hands. The piece was then dipped in waxy white glaze. The base with rim inside was glazed too. Three small birds were also glazed and painted with blue and yellow underglaze.

When the pieces came out of the glaze kiln, a small stick was cut to fit into the prepared shoulder area. Tiny brass chains were used to hang the three small birds from the stick inside the *pajarera*. The mounted birds were easily removed so that a candle could be placed on the rimmed base and piece used as a cut-out lamp.

Nun Candle Holder

The series of pencil holders (see Chapter 10) that began with the squashed owl suggested yet another piece. After the cowled figures of the padre, the next idea that came to mind was a veiled nun. To make the nun, an open-bottomed, bullet shape was thrown on the wheel. A base with an inside rim was made to mount the nun and hold a candle (Fig. 5-21).

Near the top of the bullet shape an oval opening was cut. An oval button of clay was indented, with the fingers, to make eyes and at the same time leave a ridge of clay for a nose. The face was pressed on the inside back wall, so as to be seen through the opening, after the surface was scored and liquid clay added.

Mouth, closed eyes, and praying hands were all drawn into the soft clay with a pointed stick.

A small wire loop tool was used to outline the nun's habit. A wood drill was used to make holes in front to simulate a rosary with a cross. (A slim stick might also be used). After the bisque-firing,

Fig. 5-23. Elaborate overall design of stylized cat and sun face (on the opposite side of vase) in the sgraffito technique. Design was incised into the dry glazed surface with a sharp-pointed dental tool. 8½ inches tall; covered top with handle.

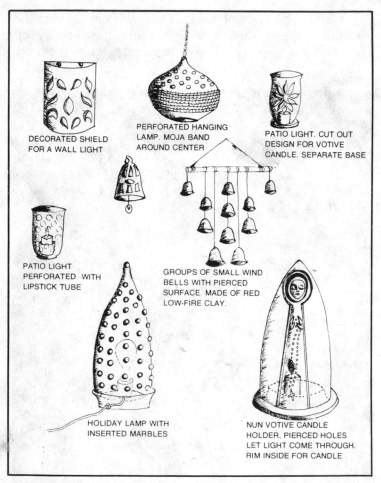

DECORATED SHIELD
FOR A WALL LIGHT

PERFORATED HANGING
LAMP. MOJA BAND
AROUND CENTER

PATIO LIGHT. CUT OUT
DESIGN FOR VOTIVE
CANDLE. SEPARATE BASE

PATIO LIGHT
PERFORATED WITH
LIPSTICK TUBE

GROUPS OF SMALL WIND
BELLS WITH PIERCED
SURFACE. MADE OF RED
LOW-FIRE CLAY.

HOLIDAY LAMP WITH
INSERTED MARBLES

NUN VOTIVE CANDLE
HOLDER, PIERCED HOLES
LET LIGHT COME THROUGH.
RIM INSIDE FOR CANDLE

Fig. 5-24. Examples of items with decorated surfaces.

wax resist was painted on the face, hands, cross, and details of the
habit, as well as the bottom of the bullet shape and base. The piece
was then dipped in bronze glaze.

The serene face and string of holes catching the light from the
flickering votive candle created a glowing picture.

Cut-Out Lamp

Wind bells, votive candle, patio lights, and hanging lamps are
all marvelous projects that involve cutting out patterns on wheel-
thrown forms. The festive holiday lamp shown in Fig. 5-22 is not
really difficult to make. Begin by throwing an open-bottomed

tapered cone on the wheel. Throw a second flared bowl shape at least a half-inch wider than that of the cone you have just thrown. You can vary these shapes to your own taste.

When the cone is firm, cut holes clear through and remove the cut clay. (A lipstick tube cover is perfect for this. The solid end can be cut off on grinding wheel, leaving a sharp edge on either end, so clay plugs are easily removed as you continue punching out series of holes.)

Two holes should be cut inside the base to allow for electric wire and a small off-on switch to be inserted. After these two pieces have been bisque-fired, marbles are glued into the holes.

Fig. 5-25. Elegant double-handled covered urn has overall pattern with sun and flame motifs. Reduction firing produced a patina on raised portions of the piece.

Fig. 5-26. These rectangular planters were made from slabs about ¾ inches allow for carving with a Kemper R2 ribbon tool. Iron oxide stain was used on the outside; waxy white on the inside. Iron oxide was stippled onto waxy white surface, using a sponge, before the Cone 10 reduction firing.

Use any good white glue such as Elmer's or Wilhold, or epoxy. The lamp shown was sprayed with gold enamel.

SGRAFFITO TECHNIQUES

This stoneware container, 8½ inches tall, is an example of *sgraffito,* or scratched surface decoration (Fig. 5-23). After bisque-firing, the pot and lid were dipped in waxy white glaze.

The entire surface of both container and lid was thickly coated with a wax resist emulsion, using a wide, soft brush. The waxy surface was allowed to dry overnight. The following day, a design was drawn on the dry waxy surface. The design was then carefully incised into the wax, using a sharply pointed dental tool.

A soft brush was used to remove all dry wax and glaze particles when the entire surface had been carved. You can buy a *sgraffito* tool or use a strong needle tool for this work.

When doing *sgraffito,* the carved lines have to go deep enough to scratch the surface of the bisque ware. You can tell by the sound if your tool has really cut a line clear through both the wax covering and the glazed surface.

When you are satisfied that your design is complete and the carved lines are sharp and clean, you are ready to apply the stain. Prepare a solution of iron oxide and water in a small bowl. Dip a sponge into the iron oxide and pat evenly into the entire design surface of both lid and container. After a thorough *checadita* (check-up) to be sure all lines are saturated with the stain, clean entire surface with moist (not wet) sponge.

Be certain all smears of iron oxide have been removed from the waxed surface. The piece is then ready for its glaze firing.

See also Figs. 5-24 through 5-26 for other decorating ideas.

Other surface decorating techniques will be explained in Chapter 9.

Chapter 6

Throwing on the Wheel

Throwing on the wheel is a mechanical means of making a round, hollow form. The wheel is able to produce only symmetrical forms but it takes a great deal of practice and patience to acquire this skill—*forcing the clay to do what you want it to do*. A famous potter once said that to become truly expert, it requires the physical strength of a wrestler and the delicate skill of a surgeon. Some people, however, take to it naturally, and prefer it to hand-forming.

Many craftsmen prefer the individuality possible only in a handmade piece to a more symmetrical piece throw on the wheel. But there are great advantages in knowing something about *each* method. It gives you a freedom in working and in knowing you have a wide range of expression.

At *Clay in Particular* both methods are used and combined to achieve their distinctive look in stoneware. By using both wheel and hand methods, they create their most fascinating pieces. They use commercially prepared clay, de-aired and pugged, ready for use (Fig. 6-1). It requires very little wedging (Figures 6-2 through 6-4).

BASIC WHEEL WORK

You begin by centering the clay (Fig. 6-5). This will take practice and patience but will ultimately produce skill at the wheel. If you are working at an electric wheel, make sure you are seated so that the *wheelhead is at lap level*. Then, with your body tilted slightly forward, the back and shoulder muscles will support the arms which are braced by resting on the thighs.

There is a hypnotic urge for the eyes and hands to follow the movement of the clay. Resist this! The pressure of your arms and hands must remain steady until the entire lump of clay is centered. It will appear perfectly motionless. It is a good rule never to take your hands off the clay abruptly because it will become off-center. When the clay is centered, you are ready to open it up and make your cylinder.

Many teachers suggest to the inexperienced worker that he throw one small cylinder after another, then discard them. One instructor told Gonzalo that once he had perfected a cylinder on the wheel, he should try making a bottle with a neck.

"When you learn to do *that*," he claimed, "you can make anything!"

Decide before opening up the cylinder whether the piece needs a solid bottom or whether it is to be an open cylinder. As an example, the figure of the Balloon Man in Chapter 3 would not require a bottom, whereas the flower holder (Chapter 10) would

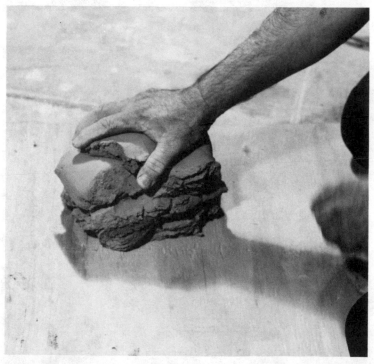

Fig. 6-1. Pugged, de-aired clay as it comes from the bag. Here the potter has cut off a few pieces of clay and is ready to wedge it (photo by Virginia Mc Intire).

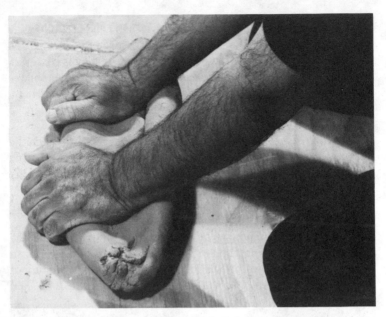

Fig. 6-2. Kneading and wedging clay (photo by Virginia Mc Intire).

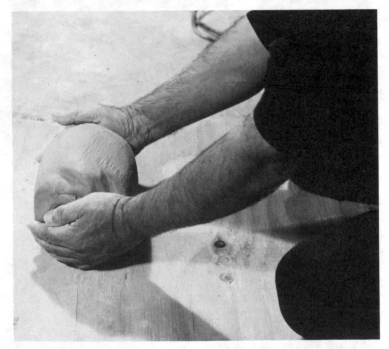

Fig. 6-3. Clay rolled into a ball (photo by Virginia Mc Intire).

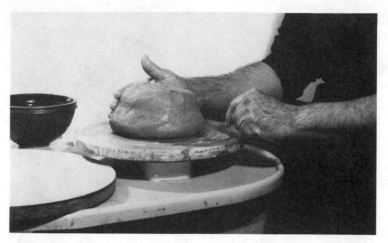

Fig. 6-4. Clay before centering.

Fig. 6-5. Centering the ball of clay (photo by Virginia Mc Intire).

Fig. 6-6. Opening the cylinder (photo by Virginia Mc Intire).

need one. If you want your piece to have a ¼ inch or 1 inch base, you will have to allow this *plus* ¼ inch or ½ inch more for the floor of your piece.

Using your thumbs, open up the centered clay (Fig. 6-6). Establish the bottom of your cylinder by pressing the clay gradually from the center *outwards* while bracing the outside. Many potters use the heel of their hand when opening up a larger piece.

Putting your left hand inside, start at the bottom; press and lift the clay upwards while using the right hand on the outside to control the shape. One technique is to double back the knuckle of your right hand index finger, making a tool of the entire side of the hand. The clay is pulled upwards slowly and steadily from the floor of the cylinder. Repeat this process until the clay walls are the desired thickness (Fig. 6-7).

As your cylinder gains height, stronger pressure is needed from the outside to control the widening of the cylinder. To form a

Fig. 6-7. Making the pot wider and taller (photo by Virginia Mc Intire).

Fig. 6-8. Using cana to shape the bottom (photo by Virginia Mc Intire).

Fig. 6-9. Smoothing the form (photo by Virginia Mc Intire).

Fig. 6-10. Collaring the top of the pot (photo by Virginia Mc Intire).

Fig. 6-11. Closing and finishing the sphere (photo by Virginia Mc Intire).

neck, *collar* the cylinder gradually with pressure from both hands. Think of your braced body as a tool to control the responsive clay. The clay must respond to the potter's will (Figs. 6-8 through 6-11).

Some people like to see the grooves left by the potter's fingers on a pot. They feel it lends authenticity to a hand-thrown piece. If a smooth surface is wanted, a potter's rib made from wood, metal, or rubber (either soft or hard) can be used. A ceramic rib tool can be made and glazed.

To remove the pot from the wheel use a wire cutting tool, which you can either buy from a ceramics supply house or hobby shop, or make yourself. Starting from the side farthest from you, and staying as close as possible to the wheelhead, or bat, cut under the clay and loosen it. Keep the wire taut as you pull it toward you. Maintaining this tension is important as you cut under the clay; otherwise you will destroy the floor of the piece. Remove the piece gradually.

COMPLETING THE PIECE

When a thrown pot is firm, or leather-hard, most potters return it to the wheel to trim the foot. This is one of the chief differences between what is *usually* done and what is done at *Clay In Particular*. At *Clay In Particular* some of the plates, bowls, and vases are finished this way. However, most are fanciful forms and figures, so conventional footing does not apply. After glazing and firing, cork or felt is glued to the plain bottom to protect furniture from scratches.

All pieces which have been assembled, or have had clay parts added, should be covered lightly and allowed to dry gradually to avoid cracks or pieces pulling apart where they have been joined. For proper drying, place the piece on newspaper, sand, or grog, so that it crawls as it shrinks in the process of drying. The pieces must be bone-dry, without a drop of moisture, before being bisque-fired.

Chapter 7

Benigno of Guanajuato

One day a man in Guanajuato ordered a special lamp base from Benigno. He was happy to oblige, but on finishing the piece discovered it was too tall for the kiln. Not discouraged, he cut the lampshade in half, making a wavy cut which gave him two sections with a scalloped edge. After firing the pieces separately, they were put back together again. They fitted perfectly.

He decorated the sections in such a way that the design on each section corresponded with the other. The wavy line looked like part of the design. It was an 'accident' with a future. It proved so attractive he decided to try the technique on other pieces. That was the birth of a cookie jar with the bird on top. This bird, too, has a story (Figs. 7-1 through 7-3).

BENIGNO AND HIS COOKIE JAR

In San Juan de Lagos there was a fair every year on the second day of February in Ferla de la Candelaria. All children were given toys, *matracas*, and whistles. The whistles, made in great quantity, were in the shape of a bird. By noon every child at the Fair had his whistle, and their chorus of cheerful tooting became the music of the fair. This childhood impression always remained with Benigno.

Here, in his own words, Benigno tells how he makes his cookie jars.

"The most popular size cookie jar takes a ball of clay weighing about seven pounds. The making of the sphere follows standard practice, opening up a bowl and closing it again into a ball, and

Fig. 7-1. Throwing the bird-form off the hump. Bird serves as handle for the jar (photo by Virginia Mc Intire).

Fig. 7-2. Removing bird-form that has been closed to a point (photo by Virginia Mc Intire).

Fig. 7-3. Attaching bird to the piece. Notice that wings have been added to the shaped bird. They are lightly detailed (photo by Virginia Mc Intire).

allowing it to dry for seven hours. At this point a small hole is made at exactly top center. This prevents the piece from developing cracks due to uneven drying. It is allowed to dry five to seven hours

Fig. 7-4. Making the scalloped cut (photo by Virginia Mc Intire).

Fig. 7-5. This picture shows the cut as lid is lifted. A small airhole should be made from inside lid into the body of the bird (photo by Virginia McIntire).

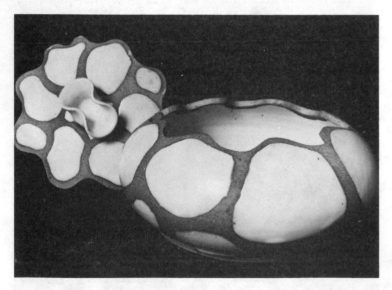

Fig. 7-6. Cookie jar by Benigno, opened up to show scalloped edges at opening; ribbon bowknot handle. Waxy white glaze and wax resist wavy-line pattern allows the rich natural color of the clay to show through.

longer before making the cut that identifies it as a Benigno cookie jar.

"Cutting the scallop requires practice. The knife used in making the scalloped cut should be thin and narrow, with a sharp point. A fettling knife is ideal. It should be ground to half its original width, making as sharp an edge as possible. An X-Acto blade, if long and narrow, might work.

"Place the sphere on a banding wheel, a kick-wheel or on an electric potter's wheel at the lowest speed.

"How do you want your lid to be? The higher the cut, the smaller the opening. If you want to use the piece as a serving container, you might want to cut it halfway down the sphere—at the widest point.

"When this sphere is rotating slowly, insert the knife. Hold it perpendicular to the surface. As it rotates, you lift and lower the knife, keeping strict control over the *angle* of the knife. This control is all important. You may have to change the up and down rhythm of the wavy line in order for it to end at the exact point where you started."

Fig. 7-7. Cookie jar by Benigno, shown to display overall design, when jar is closed. Waxy white and wax resist wavy-line design allows the natural color of the clay to show through.

93

Fig. 7-8. Design of figure and stars flows freely over the top of the lid. Decoration is painted like a wash with a Japanese brush; black underglaze over a G3 matte glaze. With a pointed implement, stars were cut through the glaze allowing fine white lines of waxy-white to show through. It was fired in a reduction kiln. The G3 matte glaze fires to a gray-white with a faint pink flush. Benigno's waxy-white bird provides a handle for the lid.

Figures 7-4 through 7-12 show the scalloping process and scalloped pieces.

MINIATURES AND RATTLES

At one time Guanajuatan potters were known for their miniatures. Whatever they used on their own tables, the potters reproduced in miniature. They ranged from primitive *casuelas* (baking dishes) to ornate European-type tea sets. People are always fascinated with the miniscule details of spouts, handles and lids (Figs. 7-13 through 7-15).

Figures 7-16 through 7-20 show Benigno throwing off the hump, opening the pots with a tooth pick-size *palito* (tiny stick). They are glazed and appropriately decorated.

You can see how small the pieces are by comparing them with the thimble in the picture.

Fig. 7-9. Egg shaped container 4 inches tall: wax resist was brushed vertically over the scalloped cut. G3 mat brown. Egg shaped container 4 inches tall: blue-green glaze with wax resist.

Fig. 7-10. Egg shaped containers 9 inches tall. Scalloped lid has bird on top. Speckled blue glaze, and wax resist.

Fig. 7-11. Scalloped lid pots based on cookie jar techniques. Right: waxy white and wax resist which allows pattern of natural brown clay to show through. Bird on top. Left: G-3 mat brown glaze, Benigno bird on top.

Fig. 7-12. On tray: Wax resist design. Dots of G3 mat on mayonnaise jar. Same technique used on the ceramic tray. Right: cookie jar with speckled blue-green glaze, wax resist design. Benigno bird on top of lid.

Fig. 7-13. Thimble in foreground shows comparative size of highly decorated plates, vases and containers.

One Christmas, when *Clay In Particular* had a booth at an art fair, Benigno made a series of what he called Executive Rattles, designed for use by "nervous executives to play with and relieve stress." They are thrown off the hump, like the bird on the lid of the cookie jar (Figs. 7-21, 7-22). They are hollow animal forms in the shape of birds, fish and other creatures with fins, wings, ears, etc., added with soft clay.

Before the forms dry, several ½ inch balls of clay are rolled between the palms of the hands and wrapped in facial tissue. This wad of tissue, with the little clay balls rolled inside, is placed inside

Fig. 7-14. Collection of tiny tea sets, vases, etc.

Fig. 7-15. Canister set. Dime shows the scale of the tiny pieces.

Fig. 7-16. Benigno forming the cone.

98

Fig. 7-17. Benigno opening up the tiny vase with a *palito*, or little stick.

Fig. 7-18. Putting a tiny vase on the bat, with spatulate end of *palito*.

Fig. 7-19. Photo shows how the miniscule detail is achieved using a *palito*, little stick.

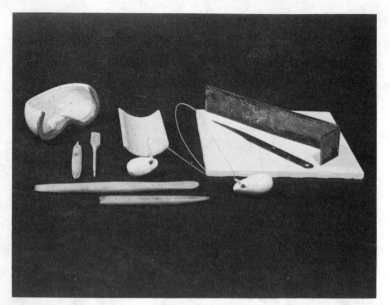

Fig. 7-20. A group of simple tools made by Benigno for his clay work.

Fig. 7-21. Fanciful animal forms, bisque-fired and ready for decoration.

Fig. 7-22. Whimsical creatures—bird and fish forms. They have been bisque-fired and ready for decoration.

the hollow form of the animal, and the bottom of the form is sealed up, leaving just one airhole.

When completely dry and given its first or bisque firing, the tissue will burn away leaving the clay balls inside to make a rattling sound. The pieces can be glazed or decorated. They are approximately 2 inches by 3 inches in size when fired.

Chapter 8

Duran from Durango: His Clay Pieces and Designs

Durango, Mexico, home of mammoth butterflies with their brilliant color and fantastic design, seems a fitting birthplace for Gonzalo Duran, whose life has always been immersed in art.

As a small boy, Gonzalo was called *Gordo* by his playmates because of his rotund figure. Hurt by their remarks, he retreated to his bedroom and began to draw. This pattern of daily sketching has been maintained throughout his life. It gave him great facility when he started to paint and later on, when he decorated three-dimensional surfaces at *Clay In Particular*.

If you have ever painted (even if you haven't), you will find it's a thrilling experience to decorate a glazed or bisque-fired piece with brush and underglaze. The bisque-fired pieces respond to a technique comparable to the use of watercolor. In a thinned-out state, you will be able, with practice, to acquire subtle gradations of color. Japanese brushes are excellent for his work, but you may find other brushes more to your liking or needs. The uncertainty of the outcome, with color changing from what you see before you to what happens in the reduction fire, may be beautiful beyond your expectations, or occasionally disappointing. But that is part of the excitement.

Design is at the very heart of Gonzalo's decoration. If you have a flair for design, you will have a great time adapting your ideas to clay. The rounded forms of pots, spheres and plates will stimulate your creativity.

DECORATING THE ROUND FORMS

Study Gonzalo's designs on the round surface of plates. He is so enamored of design that he may cover the entire piece. You can

104

make your design as rich or as simple as you like it. For the best results, the design should relate happily to the round, flat shape.

Notice the delicacy of "Girl with a Bird Nest on Her Head" (Fig. 8-1) in contrast to the "The Fiddler and The Lady" (Fig. 8-2). Look at the whimsy of "The Butterfly Man," with illustration in the center, and stylized border of flowers (Fig. 8-3).

Many of Gonzalo's designs have their roots in satire. Humor is likely to turn up anywhere in his work. If you have a sense of fun, let it all out on a coffee mug, tile or clay pot.

The roundness of the clay pots suggest endless ideas. The design may trail up and down the sides, follow the contours down the sloping sides with vines and leaves, or follow formally around them with an ethnic motif.

DRAMATIC INTERPRETATIONS IN CLAY

For a short time, Gonzalo had taken classes in ceramics at Chouinard's School of Art. So it was natural that he would one day

Fig. 8-1. Charming young girl's figure, with bird nest on top of her head, painted in black underglaze on waxy white by Gonzalo. Bird hovers over girl's head on 13 inch plate.

Fig. 8-2. Stoneware plate decorated by Gonzalo. Elaborate overall design in black underglaze on G3 mat glaze, a smooth gray surface. Although spontaneously painted, notice the interesting way in which both negative and positive spaces have been designed.

wish to enlarge his scope in clay work by throwing on the wheel. His tendency, however, was away from symmetrical pots and his inventiveness led into new avenues of design. He liked unusual forms, such as pots combined with human and animal figures, torsos and heads, sculptural forms, double-looped handles on deep-collared pots, and flamboyant containers. One of the more fanciful pieces was crowned with a cluster of nine small cylindrical pots. After throwing the main part of the piece, the separate pots were added to it with slip, the sides of the pots having been previously scored. The entire surface was then carved in a pattern of leaves with a wire loop tool. The thick handles were pulled and curved into position to support the cluster of pots. The piece was then glazed in waxy white and blue-green dribbled on each unit.

Fig. 8-3. Stoneware plate thrown by Benigno, decorated by Gonzalo; 11 inches across. Romantic design by Gonzalo features Butterfly Man surrounded by highly imaginative background with flowers, figure of a woman, moon and stars, abstract detail, stylized border of flowers. Black underglaze painted on waxy white.

Fig. 8-4. Shape ball of clay into oval with point at end.

Fig. 8-5. Hold the ball of clay in one hand. Stretch out the clay with the other. Use lots of water.

Iron oxide was brushed on heavily in some areas, and dissolved to a thin wash in others. The making of the thick, pulled handles was a departure from usual procedures and ideally suited to this Baroque container.

GONZALO'S PULLED HANDLES

Gonzalo seldom resorts to standard methods for doing his work in clay. He uses his own unorthodox approach even to the forming of handles for pots. To make these handles, you begin with a handful of clay, forming it into an oval shape with a pointed end (Fig. 8-4).

Holding the ball of clay in one hand, scoop up some water with the other hand and start pulling out the clay (Fig. 8-5). Repeat this process, gradually increasing the pressure, gently coaxing the clay into a long graceful ribbon (Fig. 8-6).

Handles ready to use appear in the right foreground of all the photos. The texture stamp at left was used to decorate base of the coiled handle after it was secured on top and bottom. Figures 8-7 and 8-8 show the pulled handle being securely attached to scored surface of the pot. Equal pressure is exerted by hand inside the pot while the other hand pinches the base of the handle onto the scored area on the outside. Figure 8-9 shows the handle being lifted into position to begin looping. An area near bottom of the pot is scored to receive the end of the handle loop (Fig. 8-10). The loop end is securely attached to the pot (Fig. 8-11). A wider and more ornate handle can be seen on Gonzalo's extravagant piece shown in Fig. 8-12.

Fig. 8-6. Stretch clay gradually. Keep your hands wet.

Fig. 8-7. Score pot for attaching handle.

HERE COMES THE SUN!

The sun has provided artists with inspiration for design through the ages. It has been painted, sketched, modeled in clay, sculptured in marble, welded in metal, worked in needle-point and applique patterns. Gonzalo uses it frequently when decorating a

Fig. 8-8. Press large end of handle into scored surface.

Fig. 8-9. Be sure fat end of clay is secure before positioning handle.

Fig. 8-10. Score the pot for placing loop of handle.

Fig. 8-11. Press down the finishing loop of the handle.

Fig. 8-12. A cluster of cylindrical pots added to the central part of a fanciful piece executed by Gonzalo. Glazed in waxy white, pattern of carved leaves over entire surface. Blue green dribbled on small cylinders. Pulled handles.

Fig. 8-13. Gonzalo Sun face painted with black underglaze on waxy white surface on mug with handle.

113

Fig. 8-14. Covered stoneware jar by Benigno, with sgraffito design made with sharp dental tool by Gonzalo. Iron oxide stain used on pattern; 8½ inches tall.

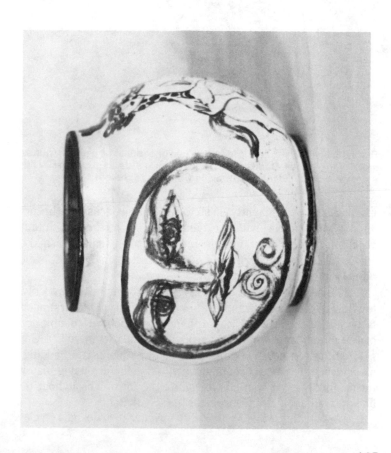

Fig. 8-15. Sun face repeats the form of this round stoneware pot. Painted in black underglaze on waxy white surface, it is complemented by two delicate figures astride animal forms in other areas of the bowl, striped in black on top and bottom.

Fig. 8-16. Stylized sun face is ideal as a design motif to be used on rounded sides of this goblet. Bands and flowers decorate the stem and base of the stoneware piece. Painted with black underglaze; height 5 inches.

clay surface. So frequently, in fact, that his sun faces have become almost synonymous with the name *Clay In Particular*. Infinite variations appear on endless forms. They are usually brushed on freely with black underglaze on waxy white, or G3 Mat, which offers a light gray ground.

The pieces illustrated in Figs 8-13 through 8-16 show only a few ideas which vary from piece to piece. Notice the burst of sun faces, six of them, which circle the collared pot with double loop handles, and the use of hearts around the collar (Fig. 8-17). Gonzalo often does near-portraits of himself as a sun face, adding a moustache. He paints spontaneously, nevertheless using his eye for design in a way that complements the form. Throughout this book are examples of Gonzalo's sun face sketches.

Think of the sun as a possibility for your own designs on clay.

Fig. 8-17. Low slung stoneware pot has a collar circled with a row of hearts. Six sun faces decorate the sides of the piece. The design is painted in black underglaze on a gray mat. Double loop handles.

Or the moon and stars. You will find them in endless variation in Gonzalo's designs. Let your imagination run free! You will be surprised at the number of ideas that will occur to you.

Chapter 9

Glazing and Decorating

When they met, the Amparáns were both manufacturers of ceramic ware. When they married, several trips to Mexico made them aware of the tremendous skill and vitality of the Mexican production potter. Their interest led them to envision the day when they might be able to bring a potter to California where he would find better living and working conditions. Would this native ingenuity be enhanced through exposure to the more technically advanced methods and superior raw materials available to the California potter? Much as they admired the accomplishments of individual California potters, they longed to find a fresh approach to the manufacture of stoneware.

The *Clay In Particular* group experiment was the result of this desire to do something different in stoneware. Their products succeeded in looking different, and nowhere more so than in their approach to glazing and decorating the surface of their ware.

At *Clay In Particular*, where the excitement was created by the design and not by the color, glazing was secondary. The pieces were often too complex or busy to introduce glaze effects. Their use of glaze has always been limited, but carefully thought out. It is dribbled, dipped into, brushed on—used in ways that set off the uniqueness of their highly individual work.

Since Joann liked to model faces and hands in detail, she didn't want to obscure those details by fully glazing the piece. Wax resist, applied to those portions, allowed the stoneware surface to remain as modeled, while remainder of the piece would be dipped in glaze. The Cone 10 firing of the piece in a reduction atmosphere assured a rich brown tone for the unglazed portion of the clay. Wax resist was used extensively in the decoration of pieces. The *Clay In Particular* look became waxy white glaze, black decoration, brown clay showing through here and there, either as the flesh tones of a figure or as a decorative motif in the surface design.

Gonzalo used to fill all the glazed portions with flowers and curlicues. This did away with the need for added colors. Already the pieces had taken on a wild rococo appearance which was rather shocking to serious ceramists.

Outside of the G3 mat brown, blue green speckled, celeste blue, temoku and bronze glazes, a greyish mat (G3 mat) glaze and the milky white (waxy white) glaze were the ones which most identified their work.

GLAZING PROCESS

The glazing of pieces is as follows: the name 'Clay In Particular' is written on the bottom of each piece with a fine brush dipped in black underglaze. The bottom of the piece is coated with wax resist. (This makes cleanup work much simpler when glazing a group of pieces.) Wax resist is applied to figure, faces, neck, and hands. Where eyes are cut out, a scrap of rolled-up tissue is stuffed into hollow eyes as well as the head cavity. Otherwise, glaze from the inside, when melted in the kiln, would flow into the eye holes, leaving a white rim which gives eyes a strange look. Wax resist should be allowed to dry completely before glazing. Usually wax is applied one day and glaze the following day.

All glazes have their own proper consistency. By using a hydrometer, the waxy white is kept at 58 degrees Baumé, being measured each time there is ware to be glazed and adding water when necessary. Most other glazes used measure around 60 degrees Baumé. When too thin, it has a dry lusterless surface. When too thick it collects or bubbles in low spots. A certain amount of experimenting is necessary. Make tests on scraps of bisque before dipping all your pieces. Glaze should dry immediately.

If you dip pieces in glaze, rather than pouring the glaze onto the piece, you will need several gallons. Waxy white is bought in quantity in powdered form. Water is added and the entire batch run through a sieve. Plastic trash barrels with lids make good containers for the glazes you use most frequently.

When glazing your ware, place your glaze vat near a large, clean surface. Keep a sponge and bowl or small bucket of water at your side. Keep a small paring knife and soft, wide brush for touching up finger marks, etc. The knife is for scraping off any thick drops that form when the glaze dries. Glazing tongs are useful to hold piece firmly when dipping. If you don't have these, hold the piece, if at all possible, with your fingers on bottom, and smooth spots where you have put wax resist or where a touchup won't be too noticeable.

After dipping, set the piece on a clean surface and, with a soft sponge, pick up beads of glaze from waxed portions. The bottom of piece is sponged (with a clean-up sponge) when the piece is dry enough to handle. Touch up any spots that have finger marks with a fully loaded brush. You might have to lay glaze on these spots two or three times and scrape off any bumpy edges with your knife. Be sure to scrape away any glaze that has collected around base of the piece. If anything, the glaze should be thinner there, or scraped back at least ⅛" from the bottom.

High decorated pieces should be carefully fired, as over-firing blurs the details. Place the decorated pieces in the cooler part of the kiln. Watch the cones carefully. Every kiln is different; there are many textbooks that will help you. The manufacturer of your kiln will be your most valuable advisor.

WAX RESIST

Wax resist emulsion is available from ceramic supply houses. It is water soluble. Paraffin wax can be melted and applied too. Wax is used on the fired ware following the same principles used in batik decoration. Whatever lines or patterns you do *not* want covered with the colored dye (in this case, glaze), you cover with a coating of wax. For ceramics, the Japanese *sumi* brushes are excellent. They hold a fair quantity of wax, yet are capable of making a very fine, pointed line. Small #00 or #1 size brights are also excellent for tiny areas. The #6 or #8 size brights will be the ones you use the most. Any larger size flat brush will do for coating bottoms of pieces. As wax requires time to dry thoroughly, try to wax your bisque pieces the day before you glaze. You will save time and materials and find the whole process faster and cleaner.

The rich brown tone of the stoneware clay when fired in a reduction atmosphere is so attractive that it became the chosen "look" at *Clay In Particular*. Carefully modeled faces and hands could be better appreciated if not obscured with glaze. The warm brown stoneware became the major part of every design. As the figures themselves are of prime importance, glazing becomes secondary. Waxy white is used as a basic creamy background for free-hand decorations.

Some underglazes which are manufactured for the low-fire hobby field prove satisfactory when applied on top of the surface of the glazed pieces and fired at Cone 10 in a reduction atmosphere. The blues, greens, browns, and one of the yellows will withstand the temperature.

All of the colors keep their brilliance when applied to the raw bisque-fired surface. As an example, the shirt of a figure had stripes cut into the surface. When bisque fired, it was painted with a pink underglaze. Each stripe was covered with wax resist and the figure glazed with waxy white. The piece emerged from the kiln with pink stripes showing brightly from between the glazed portions. Had the delicate pink color been applied to the glazed surface, it would have burned out completely.

Fig. 9-1. Gonzalo decorates his tile, which is ordinarily used as a kiln shelf, with an engraving design combining flowers and sun face with winding scroll-like stems in yellow, brown, and black.

Fig. 9-2. Large ceramic tile, 12 inches by 14 inches with underglaze decoration by Gonzalo. Lavender bull, green grass, yellow and green flowers on waxy white glaze.

DECORATING ON KILN TILE

A tile mural was ordered from *Clay In Particular*. It was to be used as a splash over a kitchen counter, with dimensions of 36 inches by 45 inches. Instead of buying the 6 inch × 6 inch bisque tiles for Cone 06 glazing and decoration, they used a 12 inch × 12 inch kiln shelf (made from highly refractory clay) which proved suitable. Not only did the kiln shelf provide a tile that wouldn't warp, but one that could be fired in a Cone 10 reduction atmosphere along with other pieces. It does not take the glaze as easily, however, as the more porous, bisque-fired clay tile.

The only flaw found in using commercially manufactured kiln shelves was that whatever glaze used, it developed a light pattern of crazing on the surface. Only if the tile is to be used as a counter where food is prepared could there be an objection. Another advantage of the kiln shelves is the wide selection of sizes. There are horizontal, hexagonal, square, round and half-round shapes from which to make a selection.

Figure 9-1 shows a tile ordinarily used as a kiln shelf, decorated with underglaze by Gonzalo. Here the artist has combined scrolls, flowers and a Gonzalo-like sun face as his motif, using a color scheme of yellow, brown, and black.

DECORATING ON A HANDMADE TILE

To make this tile, stoneware clay was rolled out to a ½ inch thickness on a slab machine and cut to a size of 12 inches by 14 inches. After bisque-firing the tile was coated with three layers of waxy white. After outlining the bull in black underglaze, the figure was filled in with cobalt blue which fired to a soft lavender. A tatooed girl looking in a mirror was superimposed on the side of the bull. A yellow sun shines down on green grass and leaves and yellow and blue flowers and butterflies (Fig. 9-2).

Fig. 9-3. Two characters who look like ancient astrologers were completely glazed in waxy white, then decorated on the glazed surface in yellow, cobalt blue, and brown. Features outlined in black underglaze. Left figure, 10 inches tall. Right figure, 12 inches tall.

Fig. 9-4. Cat made from pot thrown on wheel. Glazed in waxy white. Cat has face painted on both sides of head. Yellow eyes. A 10 inch goblet-shaped planter. Flowers on waxy white with manganese oxide in reduction firing.

DECORATING ON GLAZED PIECES

Decoration is the most obvious characteristic of the work shown in this book. When you are ready to decorate, you will find a wealth of ideas here to stimulate your imagination. There are numerous books on design to suggest other styles. But as you work, you will find this medium refreshing and as you become more facile with practice, one idea will lead you to a still better one.

Take time to study the shape carefully and decide what type of decoration it suggests to you. Pencil your design in lightly if you wish. Many skilled artists do this before applying the underglaze. If this is your first experience, start with simple forms.

Using light, clear colors will give your work a cheerful look; the more subdued tones will offer a rich effect in a monochromatic palette. For sheer drama, you can't do better than working with black and white. Black underglaze decoration used in so many of the pieces shown in this book are striking and you are not likely to tire of their simple color scheme (Fig. 9-3).

Figure 9-4 pictures unusual treatment of black underglaze decoration that is very appealing. The cat, made from a wheel-thrown form, was glazed in waxy white, with cat's faces painted on two sides. The only note of color is in the yellow eyes.

The goblet-shaped planter is embellished with a delicately painted face. Flowers and leaves trail down the narrow stem and onto the base. Painted with manganese oxide, some of the color faded into a subtle green on one side, adding to the surface interest—another "happy accident" occurring in the kiln!

Artist usually have preferences as to the type of brush they like best. Japanese brushes are excellent and many use them. Try several kinds before you decide which is the easiest for you to handle and to which you respond readily.

Chapter 10

Decorative Accessories

A decorative accessory is a very personal object. We purchase such pieces for the sake of adding a decorative note to our surroundings, to harmonize our decor, to brighten up some dull corner, or lighten a drab bit of furniture with a dash of color and design. But most of all we buy them because we *like* them, either for our own pleasure, or as a gift to give pleasure to someone else. In any instance, they are a barometer of our taste.

So it is with craftsmen who make decorative pieces. Unconsciously, their own preferences will show in the things they make.

The budding ceramist usually starts by producing small functional accessories which he refers to as *bread and butter* items. At *Clay In Particular* too, they start by making decorative accessories. Early pieces included mini-vases, trays, pitchers, bowls, casseroles, mugs, and goblets: all the things people need to hold pencils, to arrange flowers, serve food and to adorn their garden or patio. Their light-hearted approach was apparent from the start. What they made was different!

FIGURES AS FLOWER HOLDERS

In the spirit of play, Joann began to model doll-like faces and costume the varied shapes, turning them into dry flower holders. They quickly found buyers. A few of these are shown in Figs. 10-1 through 10-10. Lupe (Fig. 10-1) was one of the most popular in this series.

Gina (Fig. 10-2) was the first flower holder made in two parts. Her round sphere head was attached to a slender neck, after scoring and adding thick slip. A ruffled worm of clay under her chin gave it a lacy look. An overall pattern was scratched on the long neck.

Eyes and brows were painted with black underglaze. The hair was stained with iron oxide, and the entire piece was dipped in waxy white. Captain Nemo and the mermaid offer more sophisticated design; primarily for decoration, they do have small holes in the bodies for dry flowers. Small knee-high figures of Captain Nemo and his mermaid companion were inserted in wheel-thrown fish (Figs. 10-3, 10-4). Another larger fish-shape was made and opened on both sides to make an unusual patio ash tray or special soap dish for the bath (Fig. 10-11).

Fig. 10-1. *Lupe* flower holder. Brown and yellow flowers on waxy white. Brown crepe paper flowers with stoneware centers. Wax resist on face, hands and arms; brown hair.

Fig. 10-2. Gina is a holder for straw flowers. Her curls hide the holes made for the flowers. Waxy white glaze; wax resist on face. Facial detail painted with fine brush with black underglaze.

WAX RESIST

The warm brown, slightly rough surface of the stoneware when fired in a reduction atmosphere provided an appropriate skin tone for all of *Clay In Particular's* figures. To preserve the body color as distinct from the glazed costumes, the arms, hands, necks, bare feet, and faces were coated with a wax resist emulsion. Often the features were painted on with black or brown underglaze. Some figures had hollow cutout eyes or carefully modeled eyes, rather than painted eyes and brows.

A HAPPY ACCIDENT! PENCIL HOLDERS

When working with clay, don't be dismayed if you make a mistake. It could turn out to be a happy accident. At *Clay In Particular* one such accident gave birth to an entire line of pencil holders which could also be used as votive candle holders. It began when an owl, which had been thrown on the wheel, fell head down

Fig. 10-3. Captain Nemo dry flower holder. This 6-inch dry-flower holder may also be used as a purely decorative piece. Wax resist was used on parts of the design, allowing the natural color of the clay to come through. Waxy-white glaze surface has black underglaze decoration. Features and small detail are painted on with a very fine brush. The hole for flowers is made in Captain Nemo's hand.

Fig. 10-4. Mermaid flower holder, companion piece to Captain Nemo. Fish-form with a hole in the top for dry flowers. This is made in two pieces; the mermaid figure is attached inside the fish-form. Black underglaze design on waxy white glaze. On this form, as on that of Captain Nemo, the face is waxy white and on it, the features are painted in black underglaze. Areas of wax resist on design allows the natural clay to show through.

on the concrete floor (Fig. 10-12). In its squashed condition it looked like an Eskimo with a fur hood. A button of clay, stuck to the back inside curve of the figure, became a face. With a pointed stick, eyes, nose, mouth, and hair were scratched in and lines drawn to indicate fur on hood, jacket and sleeves. A pole and fish on a line were added (Fig. 10-13). This Eskimo figure in turn suggested a hooded or cowled robe such as those worn by a monk or padre. The padre's face had indented eyes, a balding head with a little hair above each ear. A stick was used to draw the eyes looking downward, a small mouth, and praying hands holding a rosary that trailed down the front of his robe (Fig. 10-14).

After the cowled figure of the padre, the next idea that came to mind was the veiled figure of a nun. This required a different approach. (See Chapter 4 for details on making the nun votive candle holder.)

Another pair of pencil holders that make attractive desk accessories are a seated Bolivian Indian boy and girl (Figs. 10-15, 10-16). Both were made from a low, closed pyramid shape. Heads and hats, feet and holders, were added. The girl has a single, long braid. On her back, a wheel-thrown basket-shaped container is attached. The boy has a carrier on his back made from worms of clay to simulate slim sticks of wood. Both figures have hair painted on with black underglaze. Features on the faces were modeled; hats were made from a button and a ball of clay. Hands were outlined and openings cut out for dry flowers. A slim knife blade was used to cut out the eyes. Wax resist was applied on the bottoms of the figures and on hands, feet, face, neck, and ears. A

Fig. 10-5. *Lispeth* flower holder. Girl in flowered dress is 8 inches tall. Wax resist face and arms; waxy white dress with bright blue flowers; iron oxide on hair. Holes for dry flowers were made just above the hands. Joann designed and decorated the piece.

Fig. 10-6. *Clarissa* flower holder. Iron oxide stain was used on the hair; wax resist on face and hands and the grooved stripes of her dress. Waxy white on top. Crepe paper flowers were inserted in the holes. The flowers have stoneware centers.

bold pattern was painted on the costumes with wax resist and allowed to dry thoroughly before being glazed.

The eyes and openings near the hands were filled with a small rolled-up end of tissue, so that glaze could not get inside. Both pieces were dipped in G3 mat glaze and beads of glaze on the waxed portions, carefully wiped off while still wet.

A crowned head and wings added to a squatty bell shape became an angel and a holiday best seller (Fig. 10-17). The worm arms, as used in this piece, were an integral part of the design. A *badajo* (clanger) was hung inside to make it a bell. The crown accomodates a holiday candle. (See Chapter 5 for two more tall elaborate angel bells/candle holders.)

As Gonzalo did more underglaze decoration, the pieces became more sophisticated and complex. Unusual forms, such as the three-holder candlelabra and the primitive water container (Fig. 10-18) are ideal foils for his delightfully unorthodox designs.

The candlelabra was begun by making the base and center section. The two sides, made separately, were attached to the center with slip. When the sides of the center section were opened

Fig. 10-7. *Violet* has clay worm hair, sleeves and collar trimmed with worm ruffle. Hat has texture-stamped surface. Wax resist was used on hands and face. Dipped in Chun white. Stripes are painted with a brush, using cobalt underglaze. Height 8 inches. Hole is made in each hand to hold flowers.

Fig. 10-8. *Mercedes* flower holder. Tiny dry flowers are held in carefully modeled hands held behind the back of this 10-inch figure. Long, combed strands of hair were fashioned from tapering worms of clay.

up, worms of clay were used to attach the side pieces, thus making a single unit with three holders for candles. It was the same method employed in attaching the arms to the *Dama de la Olla* (Chapter 12). The G3 mat glaze was fired to a Cone 10 reduction. The bands at the top of the holders, stars, sun face and leaf design were painted with black underglaze.

An ancient Mexican water carrier inspired the unique water container with modeled face and horns, made separately and attached with slip. The Gonzalo-like face, scrolls, and wavy lines on the horns were brushed on freely with black underglaze. Other candle holders, made in the same way as Gina, (wheel-thrown and assembled), were the regal King and Queen shown in Fig. 10-19. These had openings in their crowns large enough to accommodate oversized candles.

A 5-inch goblet, shown in Fig. 10-20, was assembled like Gina and the King and Queen candle holders from two separate pieces. The decoration was complicated as it required two glaze and wax resist applications, using both waxy white and bronze glazes.

Two-footed tumblers (Figs. 10-21, 10-22) stood 5 foot high and were decorated using wax resist, a waxy white glaze and a black underglaze design.

The group of items shown in Fig. 10-23 include the first girl made with separate legs. Two cylinders were made as legs to support the decorative torso. She was glazed with G3 mat and had elaborately decorated stockings. In left foreground is a marmalade jar decorated with a pretty face emerging from a snail's shell. Piece was glazed in G3 mat and painted with black underglaze. The 8½ inch covered jar has an all-over pattern made using the *sgraffito* method described in detail in Chapter 5. The small weedpot on the right has strong geometric insets of stylized cat, fish, owl, and butterfly on its sides (black underglaze on G3 mat).

Any one of the many useful and decorative items introduced to you in this chapter can serve as an idea springboard to launch you

Fig. 10-9. Two hollow figures attached by wedging them together. Wax resist used on faces and hands, waxy white costumes, iron oxide on hair after wax resist is dry. Crepe paper flowers with stoneware centers. Holes for flowers were made just above the hands.

Fig. 10-10. Mother and child flower holder has waxy white glaze and wax resist on face, hands, and arms. Iron oxide was used under the glaze on the hair. Crepe paper flowers have stoneware centers. They fit into holes in the figure.

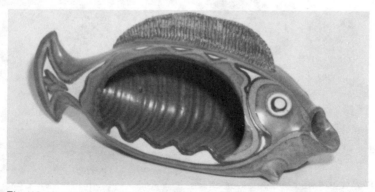

Fig. 10-11. "Happy Fish" is a shaped cylinder with a solid base, a fish-shape with one side open. Bronze glaze is highlighted with accents of black underglaze detail and waxy white.

Fig. 10-12. Owl pencil holder has a solid clay bottom. The hollow eyes were cut out and beak added. Claws and feathers were indicated with a pointed stick. G3 mat glaze was dribbled over wings. Temoku glaze dribbled on top. It was made in two sizes, 8½ inches and 4½ inches.

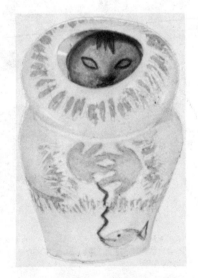

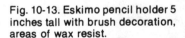

Fig. 10-13. Eskimo pencil holder 5 inches tall with brush decoration, areas of wax resist.

137

Fig. 10-14. Padre pencil holder. A button of clay was used for the face; wax resist was brushed on face, hands, rosary and outline of sleeve. The piece was then dipped in G3 mat brown.

Fig. 10-15. The Bolivian Boy with his striking wax resist costume carries slender sticks of clay on his back in a special holder. Thrown figure is 5 inches tall.

Fig. 10-16. The Bolivian Girl, hat perched jauntily on top of her head, carries a large container on her back for pencils or other stowaways. Dipped in G3 mat brown; wax resist design on her costume. Clay braid made separately and added to figure with slip.

Fig. 10-17. Mexican Angel Bell/ Candle Holder 6 inches tall. Worm arms and wings, hair-bun were added to this squat figure of angel. Black underglaze on face. The figure was turned on the banding wheel to make the wax resist stripes. Dipped in bronze glaze.

139

Fig. 10-18. Three-holder candelabra was begun by making the base and center section. The two side pieces, made separately, were attached to the center piece. When the sides of the middle section were opened up, a worm of clay was used to attach the pieces, thus making a single unit with three holders for candles. It was the same method as that used for attaching arms to the Dama de la Olla. G3 mat on Cone 10 body, black underglaze decoration.

Primitive water container. G3 mat glaze, black underglaze decoration. The design was derived from water carriers used by primitive Mexican tribes. The horns were thrown separately and attached to the body of the container in the same manner as arms were attached in Dama de la Olla.

Gina has iron oxide hair; waxy white glaze. Design on neck was made with texture stamp into waxy white glaze. Hole in the top of her head contains small straw flowers. Eyes painted with black underglaze.

Fig. 10-19. Pair of candle holders 8 inches high. The King has underglaze decoration on hands, neck and face. Waxy white glaze and wax resist. The Queen in this fanciful pair is a 9½ inches high, texture stamp design on waxy white glaze on neck; wax resist.

Fig. 10-20. Stoneware drinking goblet. White flower design on bronze glaze.

141

Fig. 10-21. Stoneware footed tumbler. Fish design, black underglaze painted on waxy white ground. Wax resist circle around fish designs.

Fig. 10-22. Stoneware footed tumbler. Black and white and natural clay design. Underglaze decoration and wax resist around flowers. Stripes at top and bottom in underglaze.

142

Fig. 10-23. From left to right: Separate leg figure from wheel, G3 mat, black underglaze decoration 6½ inches tall. Marmalade jar has a Snail Lady design by Gonzalo, outline in wax resist, letting dark brown color show through. G3 mat. 5½ inches tall. Covered jar, 8½ inches tall. Sgraffito technique, iron oxide on waxy white. (Sgraffito technique described in Chapter 5.) Small weed pot, 5½ inches tall, with elaborate cat, owl, fish and bird design circling the piece. G3 mat.

into new ways of making or finishing your own clay products. The main thing is to experiment freely and surprise yourself with what comes about as a result. Above all, enjoy your work, and you will find it gives pleasure to others.

Chapter 11

Dama de la Olla

Dama de la Olla (Lady with a Pot), shown step-by-step in Figs. 11-1 through 11-7, is begun with a cylinder thrown from the wheel. Because the figure must have a neck, it should be thrown with that in mind. After you remove the thrown form from the wheel and the surface no longer looks wet, you are ready to work. Remember that all hollow figures shown in this book require the use of both hands, working simultaneously: one hand on the inside, one on the outside.

CYLINDERS AND PUSHED-OUT FIGURES

Place your fingers in the head cavity and push in with your thumb to make two indentations where you think the eyes should be . . . about one-third of the way down from the top of the head. Use the index finger to go inside the head and push out the cheeks. Do this gradually so you won't poke a hole in the clay (Fig. 11-8).

Before you start on the arms, be sure that you position the head so that the eyes look straight forward.

Go into the cylinder with one hand, leaving the other hand free to control the shape (Fig. 11-9). With one hand inside, push out to start creating a feeling of the arms. Always do this gradually when pushing out forms. Push out an elbow, upper arm and shoulder. This can be done with the knuckle of your index finger. Push out gradually until you have shaped the upper arm. Use the same technique to shape the lower arm that is folded across the waist.

The nose is basically triangular in shape. To make the nose, start with a small triangular wedge of clay (Fig. 11-10). To secure

144

Fig. 11-1. The cone is made from centered clay.

Fig. 11-2. Opening up the cylinder.

Fig. 11-3. Pulling up the cylinder and making it grow.

and refine it, keep your fingers moist. Blend this small wedge into the surface, using your index finger (Fig. 11-11). Do not try for too much detail. For the most effective results, study the simple, primitive faces of African or pre-Columbian figures.

Now you are going to make the chin. Be sure the face is well-aligned with the center of the body. Make a button of soft clay to form a chin (Fig. 11-12). Press from inside the chin area with one hand as you model on the outside with the other.

You might wish to push out the cheeks a little, so that you can blend the cheek into the chin until your contours are the way you

Fig. 11-4. Developing the form.

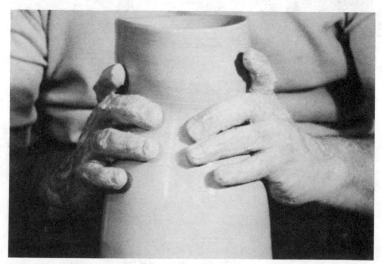
Fig. 11-5. Collaring the form for head and neck cavity.

Fig. 11-6. Completing form for neck and head.

Fig. 11-7. When surface is dry, you are ready to work.

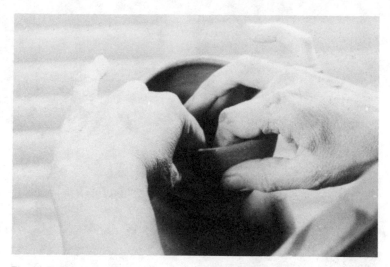

Fig. 11-8. Forming the face: eyes are pushed in, cheeks pushed from inside out.

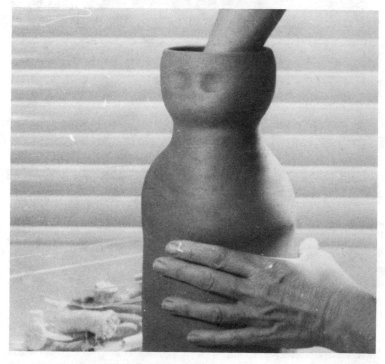

Fig. 11-9. Pushing out shoulders and arms from inside.

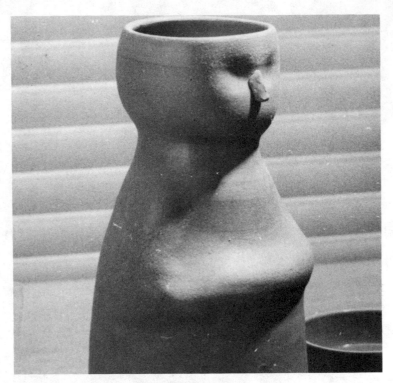

Fig. 11-10. Arms pushed out and nose added.

Fig. 11-11. Refining the shape of the nose.

Fig. 11-12. Adding on a small triangle of clay for the chin.

want them. Work the clay between your fingers, smoothing and pressing.

Decide where the ends of the mouth will be. Locate them by making a small indentation with the tip of your modeling tool. The ends of the mouth are in a direct line with the center of the eyes. To make the mouth, take two pea-sized balls of clay, roll them between your fingers, tapering them at the ends. Place these two pieces, one above the other, half way between the nose and chin. Press them gently into place.

The mouth should tuck into the cheek, not suddenly jut out from the face. Don't hurry the modeling (Fig. 11-13).

To model the upper lip use a small wooden tool. A slender wooden manicure stick will do. A smooth tip is most desirable for this delicate work. With the manicure stick, open up the lips so they are slightly apart. Keep the modeling simple.

Study the shape of the mouth. Is it in character with the rest of the face? If you want to stress the ethnic look, you won't want a small rosebud mouth; emphasize the boldness of the features.

If you wish to achieve a primitive look, don't refine the worm-shaped pieces (Figs. 11-14 and 11-15) which are suitable for such a

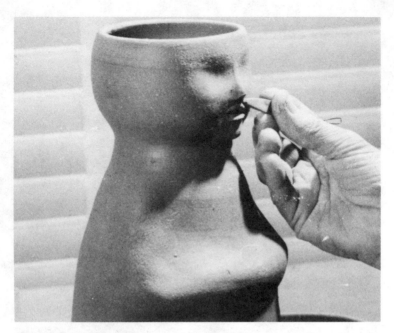

Fig. 11-13. Modeling the lips.

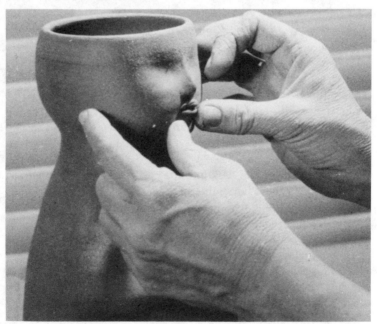

Fig. 11-14. Adding the worms of clay for the mouth.

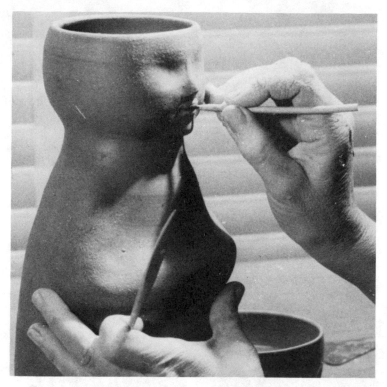

Fig. 11-15. Refining the mouth.

figure as la *Dama de la Olla*. To soften the sharper lines, use the elephant ear or cosmetic sponge (Figs. 11-16 through 11-20).

ANOTHER DAMA DE LA OLLA

Make a form on the wheel comparable to the one used for *Dama de la Olla* without arms (Fig. 11-21). On this particular figure, a smaller head was used, with a smaller opening.

On the wheel, throw two cones of clay approximately 5 inches or 6 inches long. When you cut off the cones, pinch the small ends together to make a simplified hand (Fig. 11-22). Cut the cone of clay at an angle, about 1½ inches from the larger end to fit the arms to the body.

Cut a hole at the side of the body at shoulder level. Then core deeply as shown, with a wooden stick around the hole (Fig. 11-23). After scoring the edge of the arm, apply soft clay to the shaped armhole, and open end of the upper arm (Fig. 11-24).

Fig. 11-16. Gently sponging the mouth.

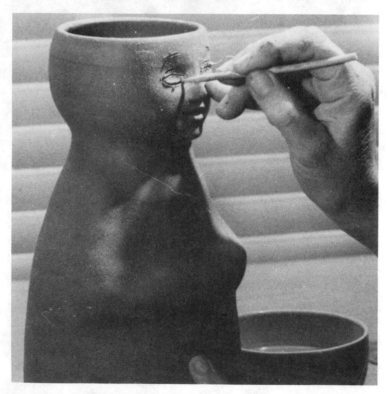

Fig. 11-17. Drawing the eyes with a pointed stick.

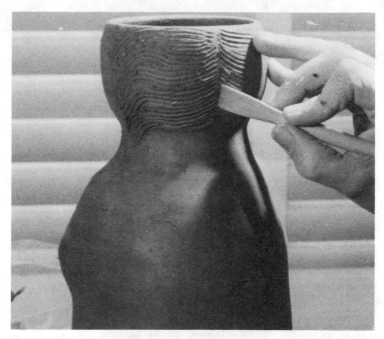

Fig. 11-18. Combing the hair from the center part with serrated tool (back of head).

Fig. 11-19. Combing hair and texturing the braids.

155

Fig. 11-20. The completed figure of Dama de la Olla may have a delicately modeled face (like the one shown here) or bolder-type features, shown in step-by-step pictures. Better try the latter, if you are a novice, at least on your first figure. If you've had experience modeling, be as sensitive and detailed as you desire. Change details of costume to complement the face of your Dama. Graceful hands and long, twisted braids were added. Figure has hole in hand for dry flowers. The pot is separate and removable.

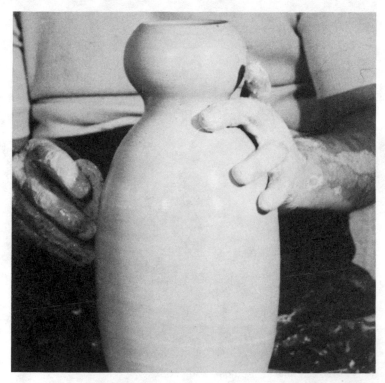

Fig. 11-21. Another version of the Dama.

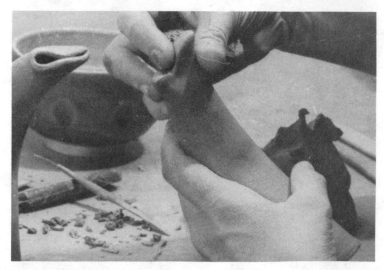

Fig. 11-22. Pinch end of wheel-thrown cone to make a simple hand.

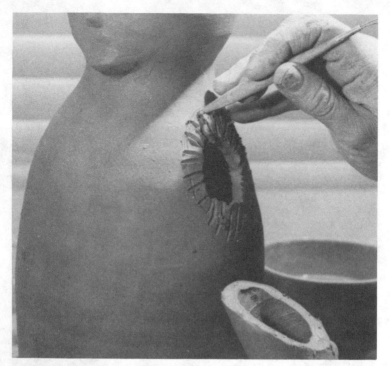

Fig. 11-23. Cut hole at shoulder, and score.

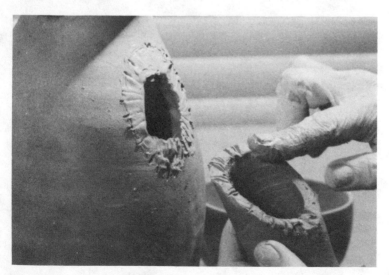

Fig. 11-24. Apply slip (soft clay) to hole and end of arm.

Hold the clay arm in your right hand and press it firmly onto the armhole. Put the fingers of your left hand inside the form and pinch the top of the armhole and arm opening together. Press firmly all the way around until solidly attached (Fig. 11-25). This eliminates the possibility of air pockets.

MAKING BRAIDS

To make the braids, roll out a 3½-inch worm of clay tapering it at the ends. It should be about 4 inches overall in length. Comb the hair texture with *dientes,* or with a heavy comb (Fig. 11-26). Fasten the braids to the head, adding slip and pressing firmly. Comb over and blend into other hair (Fig. 11-27).

You will enjoy making braids for other figures you make. Roll out long tapered worms of clay, 4¼ to 6 inches for the braids. Using a wooden tool with a serrated edge, or a wide-toothed comb, comb the clay worms. Twist two pieces together and attach the flat ends to the base of the head.

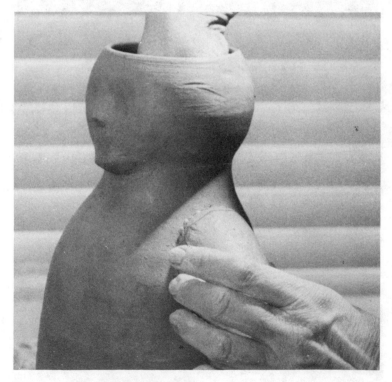

Fig. 11-25. Sticking arm onto the body.

Fig. 11-26. Making a braid from tapered worm of clay.

Fig. 11-27. Texturing braid onto head with slip.

160

Fig. 11-28. Braids in back with ribbon ends.

Fig. 11-29. Double looped braids down the back of the figure.

Fig. 11-30. Braids on top of head, simple part in back of head.

Fig. 11-31. Loose braids in front of figure. Bows at ends of braids.

162

Fig. 11-32. Bangs at front, chignon at back of head.

Comb a part down the back of the head with a stick. Starting at the part, comb the hair out toward the neck. Comb the hair from around the face, toward the back to flow into braids. The braids can be attached and smoothed firmly on to the head, then combed again to blend with the rest of the hair. Other hair styles, which are

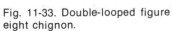

Fig. 11-33. Double-looped figure eight chignon.

attractive and ethnic, are made in the same way as shown here (Figs. 11-28 through 11-33).

To make double braids, use 8 to 10-inch worms, 1 inch thick—not too fat. Twist them together. Anchor the ends near the part and bring the ends of the other braid next to it. If the clay is soft enough, you will not need the slip.

Chapter 12

Elaborate Pieces

Throughout the preceding chapters, we have discussed various ways of forming clay pieces, and how to decorate and embellish the clay surface, as applied by *Clay In Particular's* three artists.

In this chapter we shall talk about making more elaborate pieces by combining a number of techniques to complete a single figure or interesting groups. Most of them started as wheelthrown pieces. Many of the figures discussed in this chapter are referred to as *separate leg* figures, because of the way they were put together.

SEPARATE LEG FIGURES

Paco (Fig. 12-1) was made to hold straw flowers, but soon boys with fish and one with a balloon (mounted on a length of clothes hanger) were made (Fig. 12-2). This boy with a single balloon suggested the idea of a Balloon Man selling balloons with a little boy as his customer (Fig. 12-3).

Separate leg figures can be made from wheel-thrown cylinders with heads. The Balloon Man, Paco and the clown with a ball on his head are all examples. Start your separate leg figure while the clay is still in a pliable state. Put one hand inside and push out the arm shape, starting from the shoulder area. Then push out the shoulder. After you have pushed out arms, shape the lower back and buttocks area.

With a towel or soft cloth, make a thick pad to lay the figure on as you work. This helps you protect the work you've already done on the figure. With a *dientes* tool, score the raw edges of the cuts you have just made. Brush thick slip on the scored edges and press

Fig. 12-1. Paco (nickname for Francisco). Wax resist was used on face, hands and stripes. Eyes were painted with black underglaze. Hair, pants, and shoes painted solid black. In a hole made just above the right hand, a white crepe paper flower with a stoneware center.

one edge over the other to form a pant leg. Join the entire length, using your fingers to work both inside and out. Repeat this process to make a second leg. There will be a huge gap in the middle between the legs. So roll out an oval pad of clay, ¼ inch thick.

Score the crotch area and add the clay pad, smoothing and pressing clay firmly until it fills the entire gap between the legs.

Roll out a pancake of clay about ½ inch thick. Cut two shoes that are an appropriate size for the pants legs. Score the tops of the shoes and add slip. Press the legs of the figure firmly onto the shoes. Model and smooth the shoes under the pants legs.

Cut off the rounded top of the Balloon Man's head so that his hat can be stuck on.

If you make a well-rounded separate leg figure, you might consider turning it into a balloon vendor or a vendor with a cart of lollipops or flowers. These are pieces into which you can inject some fun, even satire if you have a flair for it. Add nose, ears, or

Fig. 12-2. Group of four boy figures in stoneware. Two little fishermen in foreground, G3 mat glaze wiith black decoration. Boys with balloon and flowers, respectively, have blue and yellow T-shirts and pants, decoration on waxy white glaze.

Fig. 12-3. The Balloon Man. Two separated leg fixtures, wax resist and
waxy white glaze; decorated in Capri blue and black. The base was thrown
separately. The figures were then set on the base. When the glaze melted
in firing, they were melted to the base.
The balloons are ceramic, waxy white glaze, decorated in Capri blue and
black underglaze. Wires supporting them were made from coat hangers.

different types of moustaches. The features need not be anatomically perfect, but make them as humorous as you like. Exaggerate the features: bagginess of the pants, rakish angle of the hat . . . use as much imagination as you like.

Fig. 12-4. Organ Grinder and Monkey is a separated leg figure. Black underglaze decoration on gray mat with natural clay areas. Small monkey figure on decorated clay base. Waxy white.

Fig. 12-5. The Vendor. Cylindrical figure with separated legs. Black under-glaze decoration on G3 mat clay. Freehand brush design on hat, face, vest and pants by Gonzalo. Black and white is accented with areas of natural clay color.

Organ Grinder

Basically this figure is made in the same manner as the Balloon Man. The organ grinder's hands were modeled separately and attached to wrists and the organ. The organ was made from a sphere thrown on the wheel and paddled into a box shape. It is mounted on a tall cone. The monkey was thrown on the wheel and the small hat was added (Fig. 12-4).

Vendor and Cart

This figure is made in the same manner as the Balloon Man and the organ grinder. This particular figure (Fig. 12-5) lends itself to many variations—flower vendor, candy man and the like.

Fig. 12-6. The Vendor's Cart is a slab construction piece. Black decoration on G3 mat. Stoneware shows through where there is wax resist decoration. Holes are made in the cart for lollipops, artificial flowers, etc.

Fig. 12-7. Woman's head reflecting influences of Mayan art. Figure was painted with wax resist, the hair is waxy white, with ornate hair arrangement, combed hair.

The vendor's cart (Fig. 12-6) was made of clay rolled to about ½ inch thick. It needed four slabs of clay and a top for half of the lower part of the cart. Another box was made with four slabs and a fifth slab attached for the top. Texture stamps provided detailing on the border. Feet and wheels were carved in with a wire loop tool. The vendor and cart have wax resist decoration. They were glazed in G3 mat (black underglaze details over all of the surface).

BALLOONS

(For Balloon Man and boy and clown figures.) These are spheres thrown off the hump. A hole is pierced in the sphere when it is formed. Bisque-fired balloons are dipped into glaze, just enough to leave a round glazed dot on two sides of the sphere. This ball is then decorated with a sun face. The sphere can safely be placed in kiln for firing, resting on the unglazed portion of the sphere.

BASES

The bases for the Balloon Man and boy, and the organ grinder and monkey were made on the wheel. They are ½ inch thick and should be thrown on a plaster bat. If thrown on a non-porous bat, they will crack in the center as they dry. A few suggestions for interesting poses are little boys with hands in their pockets, ladies holding flowers in their crossed arms, and figures holding their hands behind their backs.

If you don't like to model fingers, they may be indicated by a few lines made with a pointed tool. Draw into the clay surface. Dry flowers can be placed in holes made above the hands and sleeve areas.

PROCEDURE IN FINAL FIRING

The figures were all bisque-fired and not assembled until they had been glazed and decorated. At this point, flowers were painted on the glazed base and glazed figures were set on the base in the desired position.

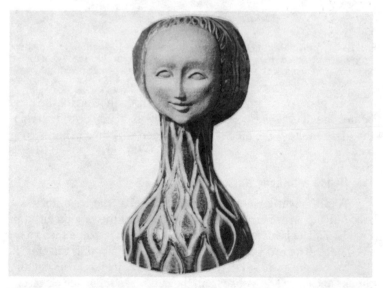

Fig. 12-8. Base and egg shape for head were thrown on wheel separately. Features on face were modeled. The head was attached to the neck area by deep scoring (scratching) and adding slip. Overall leaf pattern was cut with small loop of wire tool. After bisque-firing, wax resist was put on the entire face and in the carved lines, then the piece was dipped in Temoku glaze. Temoku is a rich, mottled copper brown c/10 glaze. Fired in reduction.

Fig. 12-9. Three elaborate figures back to back on a 16-inch plate; 3 inches deep bowl on top of their heads. Waxy white glaze on blouses, wax resist on faces and arms. Iron oxide on braids. Overall height approximately 18 inches.

All glaze was carefully removed from the bottom of the base before the figures were set on top for the final glaze-firing. When the glaze melted, the pieces were melded together in one strong piece.

Two Heads with Long Necks

A tall, slightly tapered cylinder, flared at the base, makes a graceful support for mounting a head such as the one pictured in Fig. 12-7. The head is made from an egg or oval shape thrown on the wheel. The process is much like that described in Chapter 7.

When the oval is fairly firm, from the inside push out the cheeks and chin. Add a nose from the outside, supporting clay from inside the oval so face does not cave in. Model and shape it securely. Make indentations where the eyes will be. Eyes may be drawn on, or made by adding a button of clay and placing a tapered worm of clay above and below button for lids. The mouth was made from two worms of clay. See Chapter 11 for details.

Cut the top of the neck at an angle. The highest point will support the back part of the head. Score the top of the neck deeply and add thick slip. Place the head on the neck. Press firmly. Add a worm of clay where the head and neck are to be joined. With a modeling tool or round stick, press and smooth the clay and make a gently curving line between the two parts.

With a *dientes* tool, comb hair on head, starting at the crown and following the contour of the face. Roll out long worms of clay and create any coiffure you wish. Comb the coils before arranging them on the textured head. You may add slip to the combed coils if you care to.

The glazed head (Fig. 12-8) was made in the same way as Fig. 12-7. This head, however, was made from a larger sphere; the face was modeled carefully and the remainder of the clay was pushed back to make a bonnet shape. This neck was made with a larger base. Slim worms of clay were made into delicate ovals to trim the edges of the bonnet.

A round wire loop tool was used to carve a deep leaf pattern, starting where the head meets the neck, and becoming fuller toward the bottom. After bisque-firing, the face was painted with wax resist. The entire piece was dipped in *temoku*, a mottled brown that has a reddish metallic finish when not applied too heavily.

Fig. 12-10. Turtle Man was made from six wheel-thrown pieces and assembled. Highly decorated in Mimosa, Chinese green, filbert brown, and black on waxy white. Quote is from the Bible, Song of Solomon. Length, 13 inches; 6½ inches tall.

Fig. 12-11. Triangles of clay were used in making the lion's mane which was then added to the head of Joann's "Happy Lion." The 9-inch-tall piece was made from assembled pieces thrown on the wheel. Dipped in G3 Brown glaze and wiped off, giving depth to the textured, swirling design on body made with a 'dientes' tool. Glaze gives lion an appropriate tawny appearance.

The centerpiece (Fig. 12-9) is a lavish and practical decorator item. The three figures were made like the *Dama de la Olla* (Chapter 11). While still moist, the arms were attached in a raised position. During the drying process, the one arm would invariably push forward or backward. Potters claim that clay has a "memory" meaning that clay reverts into the position it is forced into on the wheel. As a result, the arms had to be pushed forward or backward, into an extreme position, so they would dry properly.

If you intend to make any of these assembled pieces, they should be lightly covered and placed on sand or newspaper so that the bottom of the piece can crawl, since clay shrinks while drying.

If the pieces are left to dry on a non-porous surface, the wetter part is likely to stick, while the other pulls away, leaving a crack.

A shallow plate supports the figures that are placed back to back, supporting a second bowl on their heads. The bowl on top is 3

Fig. 12-12. Six thrown pieces were made and assembled for Joann's Laughing Elephant. The surface was textured with a dientes tool. The ears were made from rolled-out clay, shaped and added to the body with slip. Dipped in Celeste Blue and wiped off. 10 inches tall.

Fig. 12-13. Medieval musician made with head, arms, legs and torso thrown on the wheel. Hands, instrument, hair, nose, tunic, and shoes added. Piece was carefully assembled using soft clay to attach various parts. G3 mat glaze was used on tunic. G3 brown glaze on shoes, belt and purse; wax resist on face and hands.

Fig. 12-14. In the Moulin Rouge group, nine 4-inch figures are gathered around a table. All figures have black underglaze decoration on G3 gray mat. Tiny bottles and glasses were left free of decoration, but wax resist was used on the costumes of all the figures.

inches deep. Some of the first centerpieces assembled were glazed and fired as one unit. This proved difficult and risky. Subsequent pieces were fired separately as individual units. In this way you have five pieces to be used separately or in combinations. To use the centerpiece as shown, secure the plates and figures with wads of floral clay.

The Turtle Man (Fig. 12-10) was made from six separate wheel-thrown pieces and highly decorated in Chinese green, mimosa, filbert brown and black. A quote from the Bible was painted at the top of the turtle's shell, beginning at and spiraling out from the center. The appropriate quote is: "The flowers appear on the earth; the time of the singing of birds is come, and the voice of the turtle is heard in our land." (Song of Solomon, 2:12.) The Turtle Man is 13 inches in length and 6½ inches tall.

The lion and elephant shown in Figs. 12-11 and 12-12 were assembled from separate wheel thrown arms, legs, torsos and heads. The technique of working with one hand inside and one outside applies to all assembled figures. Surfaces to be joined are scored and thick slip is added before the pieces are attached one to

Fig. 12-15. The first Balloon Voyager lamp made by *Clay in Particular* called for the skills of all three artists. Many techniques were involved in its making. The fact that a lamp as ornate as this one was made in stoneware made it unique, as well as the elaborate concept. Lamp was 9 inches tall.

Fig. 12-16. The Balloon Voyager lamp is one of the most spectacular pieces conceived and executed by *Clay In Particular*. Its making employed a number of techniques and the skills of all three artists. This stoneware piece was hung on heavy brass chains.

another. All joints are carefully sealed and worms of clay wedged and pinched at connecting points. (For details see Chapter 11.) The figure of the musician (Fig. 12-13) was made in the same way. (See clown hands in Chapter 3.) Before making the hands, prop up the arms, pressing them into position, close enough together, so that the modeled hands will hold the horn securely.

The Groupies

It is strange that no one ever commented on the fact that these figures began at the knees instead of the feet. It was not questioned because, as a unit, the pieces stood as a well integrated design. All the Groupies fall into this category.

Nine turn-of-the-century characters clustered around a small table full of bottles and glasses was appropriately named "Moulin

Fig. 12-17. The bandwagon is elaborately decorated with yellow, blue and black underglaze designs. The piece is glazed in waxy white, and painted with black underglaze. Sgraffito technique used in scratching black off waxy white surface to leave white flowered pattern. Wax resist was used on painted details of face, hands and beards.

Fig. 12-18. Gazebo with separate lid and figures. Chinese Green on waxy white surface. Wax resist used as trim to allow the rich brown of the stoneware to show through when the piece was fired in reduction. Added figures are 7 inches high. Decorated lid with incised heart design and ceramic bowknot on top is removable.

Rouge." Hats, berets and bald heads identified the individual characters. All the pieces were finished in a G3 glaze and decorated with black underglaze, following a wax resist pattern painted on the costumes (Fig. 12-14).

Interest in the costumes of this era prompted the making of a hot air balloon with a family group in the basket (Fig. 12-15).

Going for the Spectacular: A Balloon Voyager Lamp

The Balloon Voyager Lamp is one of the most elaborate pieces conceived and produced by *Clay In Particular* (Fig. 12-16). The unique concept and execution of a lamp so intricate and appealing brought them instant recognition. The fact that it was made in stoneware made it even more unique. It stands as a perfect example of the blending of three talents.

The lamp was designed by Joann, who also modeled the small figures. The forms were thrown on the wheel by Benigno. Gonzalo did the decoration. The cut-out technique used on the balloon itself added greatly to the charm of the piece. The first Balloon Voyager lamp was only 9 inches tall.

A heart-shaped cookie cutter provided the decorative motif. In the basket a romantic couple appears oblivious to the pilot in striped shirt and plaid beret.

G3 mat glaze in the reduction atmosphere brought a pink blush to the gray surface. Decoration was black with stoneware showing through where wax resist was used.

The interest in the balloon, when made into a hanging lamp, brought custom orders for larger lamps to be hung over gaming tables. The profusely decorated balloon was high-lighted with bright yellow, green, and blue decorations on both balloon and gondola. Wax resist was used on the faces of the figures and throughout the overall design. Each custom piece varied slightly from the others and featured a heart-shaped opening, cut in the center of the gondola, so that a beam of light shone down on the felt-covered table. The gondola was hung from a lamp with brass chains. Lamps measured up to 2 inches.

Thinking about turn-of-the-century costumes brought to mind band men and band wagons (Fig. 12-17). A caliope, animal cages, a puppet theatre, and kiosks with vendors were made, plus a host of tiny World's Fair figures (Chicago 1892-93). There were also figures buying, selling, and looking—even a tiny photographer under a black cloth, holding a birdie in front of a lavishly dressed couple. Elaborate, old-fashioned Victorian gazebos all had ornate removable tops (Fig. 12-18). These special occasion pieces had

Fig. 12-19. Gazebo bandstand with musicians. Round bandstand, separate roof with cutout design and doves. Waxy white glaze covered with elaborate design on glaze, in black, green, yellow and blue. Uniformed men in black with Sgraffito detail.

Fig. 12-20. Man in the Checkered Pants is 14 inches tall. Checkers and other decorative detail painted on waxy white glaze with Capri blue and black.

many uses and encourage conversation. They usually had several small figures inside, beautifully costumed. Figure 12-19 shows band men in a gazebo and an ornate bandstand.

Circuses, fairs and festivals have always encouraged the artist's response to a colorful atmosphere. The past is fascinating! But so much is happening in the world today, it seems a shame that the artist neglects it. A vast accumulation of collected treasures and access to cultural information offers the creative-minded overwhelming choices, advantages unavailable to previous ages.

As creative workers it boils down to a question of pleasing what seems to be the ever-changing fickle tastes of the buying public. The images presented daily, even hourly, by the mass media, may stimulate us to a point of confusion. Then it is a good time to realize that beauty, originality, good craftsmanship and humor (Figure 12-20) are still sought after. They will always insure a receptive audience.

The combination of ethnic roots and traditional European art are the strongest influences at *Clay In Particular,* and the source of

Fig. 12-21. Contemporary modeled head as embellishment on an elaborate bowl has subtle appearance of a form plucked from an ancient vase. Notice delicate modeling of lips, eyes, cheeks and the floating appearance of combed hair.

Fig. 12-22. Heavily carved pot (7½ inches by 10 inches) has lush design with sun and scroll motifs. Iron oxide was applied with a brush and left thick enough to create a metallic-looking finish.

a uniquely original look. Detail from a large pot shows this influence (Fig. 12-21).

Some of the most elaborate pieces produced by *Clay In Particular* are their large, custom-made pots and containers used for planters. They are also the richest in surface decoration and the handsomest.

Observe the elegance of the group of large decorated pots shown here in Figs. 12-22 through 12-28. All of the pieces were thrown up to 1 inch thick in certain areas and patterned with texture stamps, lightly incised, embellished with modeled faces and figures, or deeply carved. (See Chapter 4.)

All pieces were glazed inside and stained outside with a solution of red iron oxide. It was allowed to settle in some areas and wiped off in others for an effective contrast.

Elegant Pot for a Pregnant Onion

Among the group of large elegant pots was the one shown in Fig. 12-23 and used as a planter for the wild cascading leaves of the pregnant onion. To make this piece, you roll out a slab of clay 1½ inches to 2 inches thick. Cover a round plastic or pottery bowl approximately 9 to 10 inches tall with several layers of dampened newspaper and wrap the whole form with plastic. This form could also be a paper box, a basket—anything that will serve as a mold over which to drape your clay. The bowl supports the shape and the dampened newspaper helps you create an irregular, free-form piece.

Making this piece is comparable to using dough in making a pie-crust. Cut out a large pie-shaped piece of clay from the slab in two or more places. Score one side of each cut with a pointed stick, then overlap the pieces together. Cutting away the surplus clay and putting the edges together forms the shape of your pot.

When the clay is fairly firm, you can begin modeling the face. Press from inside of pot with both thumbs, gradually pushing out an oval cavity that forms your face and hair area on the outside.

Make an oval of clay 1 inch thick for the face. Add this oval to surface you have pushed out, pressing the clay firmly together on

Fig. 12-23. Thrown pot by Benigno; woman's head modeled by Joann. Elaborate stamped, incised, carved and appliqued design surrounds the head with flying hair, to create a rich background. Gonzalo did some of the carving. Waxy white glaze was used inside the pot, red iron oxide was sponged onto the outside.

Fig. 12-24. Two deeply carved pots with sculptured busts. Pot on left measures approximately 10 inches by 11 inches. Vase on right, 12 inches by 6½ inches. Simulated brick texture in upper part of vase, behind figures. Bronze glaze on the inside of both pieces, which were heavily stained with iron oxide.

Fig. 12-25. These ladies' heads grace the sides of a heavily stained cachepot. Serpentine design unites the two heads on opposite sides of the elegant piece (14 inches by 15 inches). Iron oxide outside only.

both sides. Keep in mind the shape of the face as you press and mold the clay. Be sure no pockets of air are trapped when you join the two clay pieces. Then you start modeling the face, neck, etc. Press in eye areas. Add a triangle of clay for the nose and two clay worms for the mouth.

For the hair, roll out tapered strands of clay pressing down each one before adding another. With the *dientes,* comb the hair following the contours of the face and let the strands flow as naturally as possible from the head.

Adding clay to clay must be done carefully, so that no air pockets are left. To make certain this won't happen, poke the modeled parts from inside the face with a needle tool; riddle it with holes. They won't show in the fired piece.

Fig. 12-26. Detail of woman's head on elaborately decorated stoneware pot by Joann. Head is surrounded by carved and incised design. Hair is combed, features modeled; eyes made with end of pointed stick or sharp tool.

Before the piece was dry, a metal scraper was used to scratch the entire surface. The scratchy particles of the grog, (ground up fired clay) created a rough, interesting texture.

After a slow bisque-firing at Cone 10 reduction, the piece was stained with a solution of red iron oxide, painted on with a brush. The surface was highlighted by sponging off the stain.

Modeling is a study in itself. You can take classes in modeling and read books on it; on the anatomy of the face, the bone structure. If modeling a realistic face is beyond you, you might try a

Fig. 12-27. Smiling face of young girl, whose hair swirls among a pattern of textured flowers (12 inches by 10 inches). Turquoise glaze inside, iron oxide on outside, wiped off to highlight the features.

190

Fig. 12-28. Beautiful butterfly hair style, 12 inches by 11 inches. G3 mat glaze inside, stained with manganese dioxide on the outside. Face wiped off to highlight the face. Sides of the piece are covered with elaborate decoration, carved and textured.

primitive-type face; a masklike design would be appropriate on this type of large pot. Study the face on the *Dama de la Olla*. The simplified features are very effective.

Chapter 13

A Few Thoughts on Marketing

Many workers in clay produce pieces purely for the fun of doing it and the sense of achievement which is bound to accompany such effort. That is a happy end in itself. You will have the pieces around for the enjoyment of your friends and family. (Your family may do a little forgivable boasting. Enjoy this indulgence, it's healthy.)

You will discover that frequently friends and relatives will want to buy what you have made or ask you to make a special piece. A demand for work often spurs the budding ceramist on to producing a larger quantity, and before you realize what has happened, you're in business—right in your own backyard.

You may rally to the idea of a small business within the confines of your bedroom-kitchen-spare room-studio. You may even become excited about selling to specialty shops or decorators. Unless you have a friend who is a salesperson, or a manufacturers' representative, who will do the selling? Probably, *you!* The producer is often the best salesman. There is something about a personal contact that pleases the buyer of a small shop. He is talking to the artist, face to face. Who can tell him all he wants to know about the product if *you* can't? It often establishes instant rapport, and a new account is opened.

Unless you are thinking in terms of quantity production, department stores are *not* usually a good place to start. You get lost in the general shuffle of hundreds of commercial manufacturers who are able to produce similar (if not as attractive) art objects to yours. The best places for the home-potter or ceramist are the small gift shops, specialty shops, patio and garden shops and the decorating trade. The latter is mostly concerned with larger pieces such as lamps, planters and the like.

Don't worry about the fact that you've never done this before. Your very naiveté may be a plus with a buyer who is used to a slick commercial approach. You may also find that you enjoy selling. Some artists are natural salesmen, but not all of them. If you like people, however, you are bound to make an impression on a prospective buyer and a dent in his budget when he writes up your order. That is one thing you *must* insist on—a signed purchase order.

At *Clay In Particular* it was Joann who first did the selling. She has a great deal of enthusiasm for *Clay In Particular* products. And you can't beat enthusiasm when it comes to selling.

You may have a similar nature and become successful in selling your own work. But the problem is always *time!* Selling takes time and patience to establish accounts and so does your creative work. So where do you look for someone to do it for you?

It is possible you already know such a person who is willing to take on a new line, if it's lucrative enough. But the best recommendations come from people in the business—the same people to whom you've been selling. Salesmen and representatives selling various kinds of merchandise call on them constantly. They know such people, the lines they carry, what they *like* to sell—and that's important. The buyers also know the reputation of the salesmen. Are they careful about accounts they sell to? Do they have integrity—deal fairly with accounts and manufacturer alike? Are they honest? News in business circles, like in everything else, travels.

When designing and selling began to compete for her time, Joann began thinking in terms of a representative, one with a showroom that is conveniently placed, and is known to the buyers. A photographer who liked the *Clay In Particular* products first spoke to her about Brian Barlow. When she called him to make an appointment she had no idea that he was one of the most reliable representatives in Los Angeles. He also had taste, and through the years had established an enviable list of architectural firms and interior decorators as clients. Their first interview proved a complete meeting of minds.

"She was friendly and outgoing," Mr. Barlow assured us, in speaking of Joann. "People like her. Her nice, outgoing feeling creeps into her work. I have to like both the work and the artist. Her work had instant appeal and we began selling it right away."

Previously, Barlow had tried selling the work of two other well-known ceramists but the partnership combination of people and pots never worked. He has to be really enthusiastic about what he sells.

And where do you find a Brian Barlow? Business associations, furniture associations, the groups of professional decorators. The Better Business Bureau can assist you in finding reputable people.

As you work and get to know your field, and others engaged in the same work, you'll meet the people who will be helpful.

It is very much like making ceramics—you learn as you work. And, as always, experience is the best teacher.

Chapter 14

Clay In Particular Gallery

At this point, you have observed through text and illustration that each of the artists involved with *Clay In Particular* is a designer-craftsman in his own right. You have seen in this book a sufficient number of pieces made by each artist to recognize certain individual tastes and tendencies. Humor, fantasy, whimsy, spontaneity and original ideas abound in the work of Joann, Benigno and Gonzalo. Although they frequently create pieces independently, or accept commissions independently, their more elaborate and many of their handsomest pieces are a result of combined efforts.

Many ceramists are strictly solo workers; others will work well in collaboration. You may want to blend your talents with kindred souls. It is stimulating to work at a project with other creative people.

It is our hope that this book may encourage you to experience the fun and satisfaction of adapting some of the ideas shown here to your own concepts, and to extend your designing skills in clay. To further fire your imagination, we've included here a collection of *Clay In Particular* stoneware. The techniques used in their making has been detailed earlier. Enjoy!

Fig. 14-1. Benigno threw this lamp base which was then bisque-fired and dipped in a vat of waxy white glaze. Gonzalo painted the freehand decoration in black underglaze over the unfired waxy white. It was then fired to Cone 10 in a reduction kiln. It was mounted on a round, wooden base, finished with an ebony stain. The base stands 12½ inches tall, is 8½ inches wide at its broadest point. It is striking when topped, as this one is, with a brilliant red shade in raw silk.

Fig. 14-2. Stoneware decorated dishes with fanciful designs by Gonzalo painted in Capri Blue underglaze on a waxy white surface.

Fig. 14-3. Decorated pot thrown by Benigno has a ruffled top. The pot has a glazed interior in bronze color. Gonzalo painted black elongated mermaid design on waxy white strip. Strip was painted on with waxy white glaze with a heavy brush.

Fig. 14-4. Two three-branch candelabra were dipped in waxy white; black underglaze decoration. The pieces were made separately and added to the center form with slip. All fired at Cone 10 reduction.
(Rear) 12-inch-by-16-inch Star motif was used with sun face on central branch, scrolls, and leaves on smaller branches. Bands of black near rim.
(Foreground) Smaller branches combine stylized flower design with sun face and stars on center branch.

Fig. 14-5. Benigno threw these two rimmed plates and cookie jar with bird on top. Gonzalo decorated both dishes, with sun face and man on bicycle motifs in black underglaze. Striking leaf design in black on waxy white, wavy line in center showing another strip of wax resist. Design on cookie jar was painted by Benigno.

198

Fig. 14-6. A. Deep collared stone-ware vase, 10 inches tall, that flares at bottom. Sun face and stylized heart design emphasize the curved bottom of piece. Double loop handles carry stripe motif. Black underglaze brush-work on G3 mat. Light gray ground. B. Small vase with sun face in the center of one side. Leaf design surrounds it. Narrow neck. Height 7½ inches.
C. Fish-form container with open sides. Gonzalo adds a sun face on this purely imaginative creature. Length 11 inches.

199

Fig. 14-7. Umbrella stand (22 inches deep, 11 inches across). Gonzalo Duran illustrates an Edward Lear limerick all around the surface of the waxy white piece. Painted with black underglaze and fired to Cone 10 reduction. Stand was thrown on the wheel by Benigno Barron.

Fig. 14-8. This basket had ribbon scrolls added to the feet. Band at top and loops at lower part of the piece insure support for the loosely placed, vertical ribbons (11 inches by 11 inches).

Fig. 14-9. Shallow bowls with rims made and decorated by Benigno Barron.

Fig. 14-10. Pot with a ruffled top by Benigno (6½ inches tall, 7½ inches across). Blue-green glaze; flowers painted on a wide band of waxy white glaze.

Fig. 14-11. This Benigno pot with a wax resist flower design is 14 inches tall and 12 inches across. The petals were filled in with waxy white and covered with wax resist. The entire piece was then glazed with G3 mat brown. Delicately incised design on body of the pot makes an interesting contrast to the bold white floral pattern, rich in color and texture.

Fig. 14-12. The natural color of the clay shows through the wax resist design on this 14 inch tall covered jar with gray mat glaze. Accents of brilliant turquoise used on scroll design, handle to the lid of the jar, and around the collar, add a lively color note.

Fig. 14-13. *Particularitos*-Little Particulars by Benigno (from 2 inches to 3 inches tall) were dipped in assorted glazes—some solid colors, and others with wax resist designs.

Fig. 14-14. Lady in flowered dress by Gonzalo (15 inches high). G3 mat glaze. Elaborate overall decoration in Capri Blue and black underglaze.

Fig. 14-15. *Tres Marias* (Three Marias). Waxy white glaze, wax resist.

Fig. 14-16. Elaborate pot with modeled head used as planter.

Fig. 14-17. This is a custom piece, made for a fountain. A stream of water comes up through the center of the carved cylinder to cascade over these figures that are mounted on top of the cylinder. Photographed in its bisque-fired state. Figures have pastel wash of underglaze and colorfully decorated costumes. They will be fired at Cone 05, which allows the decoration to be more colorful. Finished assemblage will measure 16 inches tall.

Fig. 14-18. A pair of 20-inch stoneware figures. Low relief, clay on clay, decoration on textured costumes of women's figures.

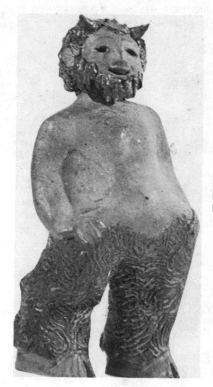

Fig. 14-19. This laughing satyr was made with opened mouth and eyes. Hair, horns and tail were added. Wax resist was used over the body. It was then dipped in mottled brown glaze (11 inches tall).

Fig. 14-20. Profile of laughing satyr.

Fig. 14-21. Clown balancing a balloon on his hand is a cylindrical figure with separated legs. Figure has brushed-on detail painted in black underglaze on waxy white. Wax resist on face, detail in black underglaze. The revolving balloon is mounted on a wire, decoration painted in Capri blue on waxy white glaze.

Fig. 14-22. Joann's modern cat sculpture in clay. Compare to ancient Egyptian cat sculpture pictured in Introduction. Either cat form would be comfortable in a contemporary setting.

Glossary

Note: Many of the terms used in this glossary will be known to readers who are familiar with clay. In some instances, however, they are used in a different way to describe our specific procedures.

applied clay: Clay added to a clay piece to enhance or enrich a surface.

bat: A disk or slab of plaster of paris or casting plaster to support ware being made or dried. Absorbs moisture from wet clay.

bisque: Clay that has been fired once before being glazed for a second firing.

bisque-firing: A first firing, (cone 010-05), before glazing and firing a second time to a higher temperature.

bisque-fired form: A piece thrown on the wheel for the specific purpose of draping clay over it.

clay: A combination of natural decomposed substances and minerals which, when water is added, become plastic enough to shape. Hard and durable when fired.

clay slabs: Clay that has been rolled, thrown or pressed into a flat slab. Usage determines thickness of clay.

combing: A method of creating texture with an actual comb or other tool with serrated edge. Used for hair or fur on figures.

cone: Pyrometric device for measuring kiln temperatures. Made from clay and fluxes, they are triangular in shape and are placed in front of a peep-hole in the kiln to bend at a given temperature. Cones are numbered according to their melting point. In this book you will find references to cone 10 and cone 06, high and low temperatures respectively.

cracking: Caused either by fast drying, careless joining of one clay part to another, or adding a too wet clay to a dryer piece or visa-versa.

crazing: Unplanned crackling in a glazed surface caused when clay body and glaze are not compatible. Not to be confused with a deliberately planned crackle-glaze.

cylindrical forms: Basic wheel-thrown form from which most of the items in this book are made.

dipping: Immersing bisque-fired pieces in a large container of glaze. This is the only glazing method used for the items shown in this book.

drape: A method of making a piece by draping slabs of rolled-out clay or clay ribbons over a mold-form.

epoxy: A durable cement useful in repairing cracks or defects; also for mounting figures, etc. Grog or color can be mixed with it.

glaze: A coating of glass which is made from finely ground minerals and applied on bisque-ware by dipping, brushing or spraying. Under heat, the glaze melts to form a glass-like surface. Glazes referred to in this book are:
Blue chun—Smooth, glossy, bright mottled blue-violet to red-violet in reduction firing.
Blue-green speckled—Deep, semi-mat with dark, iron specks.
Bronze—Antique metallic yellow with black variations.
Celeste—Traditional blue-mat.
Chun white—Glossy, brilliant white. Exquisite effect when used on porcelain clay body.
G-3 brown—Mat nut-brown mottled with yellow.
G-3 mat white—Off-white, almost gray. Non-shiny, it often shows a pink blush in reduction firing.
Steel blue—Semi-mat, medium gray-blue. Combines well with other glazes for dribbling, etc.
Temoku—Brilliant copper-brown mottled with black.
Waxy white—White, fat opaque glaze with a slight sheen. Excellent for holding a decorated surface in reduction firing.

glazing: See *Dipping*.

greenware: Term for finished ware before first firing.

grog: Clay that has been fired and crushed. Added to the clay body, it reduces shrinkage and cracking. Produces an interesting surface texture.

kiln: (Pronounced *kill*) A furnace or oven for firing clay ware. Should be constructed to withstand a minimum temperature of 2000°F.

kiln shelves: Made from highly refractory fire-clay that matures between 2500 F and 2700 F. Used to support ware during the firing process.

maquette: Small scale model for a larger work. The artist's sketch or idea in miniature.

mat (matte): A smooth, un-glossy or dull surface as opposed to a shiny finish.

mold-form: Any form over which clay can be draped to shape a piece. Used with a layer of plastic to keep clay from sticking to the mold-form.

pinch pot: A simple, primitive method for forming a hollow shape by hand.

plaster of paris: (casting plaster) Powdered gypsum compound which hardens when mixed with water. Used to make bats or molds for reproducing slip cast ware.

porcelain: A non-absorbent, hard clay body which fires smooth, white and translucent.

pottery: Earthen ware that fires about cone 08 to 2. A studio or building where pottery is manufactured.

pugged, de-aired clay: Clay that has been mixed in a pug-mill which blends the dry clay and water and extrudes it in a pliable, air-free condition, ready for use. Usually packaged in plastic bags weighing 25 lbs. Available through ceramic supply dealers.

reduction: A smoky firing in which the fuel is not completely burned because the oxygen has been muffled. This type of firing deepens and enriches the color of the clay body.

ribbons: Clay strips, cut from rolled-out clay up to ½ inch thick; used for ribbon baskets and containers.

score: To dig or scratch deeply into the clay surface where another clay part is to be added.

sculptural: Modeling or carving forms on clay surface to achieve a high or low relief; Heads or figures added to the thrown or slab formed piece.

sgraffito: Decoration by scratching through a coating of glaze or underglaze to expose the contrasting color of the surface underneath.

shrinkage: Contraction of clay in firing or drying.

slip: Clay made liquid with water to the consistency of heavy cream. Used for attaching clay pieces to one another and for pouring in plaster molds to reproduce quantities of a given item. Also called *moja* in this book.

stain: Body colorant and decorative wash. Some pieces in this book are stained or decorated with red or black iron oxide, copper and cobalt oxides and manganese dioxide.

texture stamps: A method of texturing damp clay by impressing a design into it. Designs can be carved in clay and fired. Plaster or wood can be used also.

throwing: Forming pots on a spinning surface powered either manually or electrically.

transparent mat: Non-glossy yet transparent whitish glaze through which an underglaze design can be seen as through a delicate mist. Applied on decorated bisque-fired ware.

underglaze: As the name implies, these are colors painted on bisque-ware and covered with a transparent glaze. In this book, bisque-fired ware was glazed and, when dry, decorated with underglazes. Waxy white and G3 mat are the favorite glazes. Blues, browns, black, some greens and yellows can withstand the cone 10 reduction firing.

wax resist: Specially prepared water soluble wax solution. Used in decoration or to shield portions of the bisque-fired ware from being glazed. Paraffin or crayon can be used also.

wedging: Beating, cutting and kneading clay to remove pockets of trapped air and homogenize entire mass before throwing on wheel or constructing by hand. Commercially sold pugged, de-aired clay needs very little wedging.

worm: Term used in this book to describe small coils of clay rolled out with the fingers to make hair or other small details.

Index

Edited by S.H. Mesner